How to Be Irish

Uncovering the Curiosities of Irish Behaviour

ttery

ORPEN PRESS

First published in 2011 by Orpen Press
Lonsdale House
Avoca Avenue
Blackrock
Co. Dublin
Ireland

e-mail: info@orpenpress.com
www.orpenpress.com

Reprinted 2012 and 2013.

ISBN: 978-1-871305-24-1
ePub ISBN: 978-1-871305-41-8
Kindle ISBN: 978-1-871305-42-5

A catalogue record for this book is available from the
British Library.

Printed in the UK by MPG Books Group Ltd.

Preface

This is an anthropological guide to how to be Irish. You never know when such knowledge may be needed in an emergency. If you are daft enough to really want to be one of us, if you have lived abroad so long that you have forgotten how, if you are planning a holiday amongst us, or if you are already one of us and are just curious, you may find it useful, maybe even life saving.

The job of the anthropologist is to uncover the curiosities of behaviour by providing a lens through which the social and cultural characteristics of our shared behaviour can be seen. In general, I am interested in what we actually say and do, rather than in what we think we say and do or what we would like to say and do, but don't. I am also interested in what we say we think, but usually don't.

Any study of Irish behaviour has to pick and choose its subject matter. I have picked those aspects of life in Ireland that give me the most pride in being Irish: the things that make us different and the stuff that helps us moan.

Many visitors to Ireland think we speak English. Some even spend years here before they realise that we don't. In this book you will come across several instances of Hiberno-English – the language we speak which is confusingly like English but is in fact entirely different. This vernacular, which has never been formally translated into English, makes understanding us difficult and becoming one of us very difficult.

Hiberno-English differs from English in several significant ways. First, it allows us to say one thing but mean something entirely different. While this linguistic effect causes us to appear hypocritical to outsiders, it actually makes us innately ironic. We resist committing ourselves in language because we are cagey about anyone knowing us, including outsiders. Our Hiberno-English dialect allows us to live and act in a sea of ambiguity that perfectly suits our collective purpose. Second, speaking Hiberno-English lets us look like we are absorbing English-based global culture. In fact it helps us to circumvent most of the outside world. In this way, we can appear urbane but remain fundamentally traditional. Third, Hiberno-English is closely related to the Irish language. Like Irish, it is a language of hyperbole, guilt and, perhaps most importantly, romanticised misery. By being forced to read *Peig*[1] in Irish in school, we learn how to be miserable in two languages. I am not trying to explicitly contribute to our extensive canon of misery literature, but I often find myself adopting that mode because it is such fun.

It is practically impossible to define in one book what it means to be Irish. I asked an eight-year-old Irish girl what she thought being Irish meant. Typically, she was wearing an over-sized wig of traditional red ringlets and a highly decorated step-dancing costume with a billion sequins at the time. She told me without hesitation that Irishness was 'cakes, biscuits and green' – not everyone's idea but as good as any in the circumstances. Few eight-year-olds know that our national colour is blue, but who cares? Green is nice too. For demographic balance, I asked an elderly woman,

---

[1] The autobiography of Peig Sayers, who lived on the Great Blasket Island in the first half of the twentieth century. Don't worry, it's not the last you'll hear of her in this book...

also wearing an equally unconvincing red wig, what she thought Irishness meant. She said, 'saints and scholars and Tayto crisps...oh...and Cadbury's chocolate'. I won't try to provide a definition of Irishness, but I would like to add Denny's sausages, Barry's Tea, Kerrygold butter, Clonakilty Black Pudding, and Kimberly and Mikado biscuits to the list of the dietary definition of Irishness. Perhaps we are what we eat...

On approaching most of my informants for help with shedding light on Irish behaviours and habits, the first things most of them offered me were their ideas on what needed to be done urgently to save the country. I find it interesting that so many of us feel a need to fix or improve us. I am not one of these people because I can't decide what is wrong with us or what a solution would look like. In any case, what you won't get from an anthropologist is a solution to a problem. You won't even get the problem, because anthropology is principally about describing and explaining behaviour rather than judging it. However, it does celebrate behaviour in all its diversity. It is my job as an anthropologist to describe us the way we are, rather than the way we should be. I leave the task of saving us to a higher authority than me.

Anthropology is the art of gathering and processing information. There are many techniques available for doing this. We take what is called a *qualitative approach*, which means that we will use any type of data except statistics, because we are not barefaced liars. Though many anthropologists wouldn't admit to the complete repertoire, our methods include not just the standard participation and observation, but also impersonation, solicitation, stalking, fibbing, imagination, making stuff up to fill gaps, begging and exaggeration. Different methods produce different results and my anthropological approach is to use as many techniques as possible to highlight the complexity and wealth of Irish culture. I have begged, spied, hung out and participated, knocked down my house, got a job, attended funerals and weddings, joined a political party and drank in many pubs – all in the interest of science.

Anthropologists, like detectives, are very dependent on what we both call informants. Traditionally, we anthropologists trust our informants out of a professional respect for their co-operation and believe everything they tell us. It is not in the anthropological handbook to cross-examine one's informants and demand, 'Did that really happen?' because that would be upsetting for the informant. It is a golden rule of anthropology not to upset anyone; as a profession, we are the acme of good manners. So in this book I am giving it to you just as I got it from my many very helpful sources. I believe that those narratives related to me in the pub are especially true.

Where Irish families are involved we need to seek professional help, so I consulted a psychiatrist. In Ireland it is handy to have easy access to a psychiatrist. Like most commentators, he blames Irish mammies for all of our ills. But much contemporary psychiatry is based on the theories of Sigmund Freud, the Austrian father of psychoanalysis. It may be the case that mammies are the root of all evil in Austria, I don't know. But it is unfair to blame Irish mammies for everything when their only obvious failing is to love their sons a little bit too much. Thanks, Mammy!

I am grateful for the efforts of my informants and I would like to publicly thank them. However, it is also customary for anthropologists to change the names of their informants, following the mannerly principle of protecting their anonymity. But changing their names makes it difficult for me to properly thank everyone, so I have come up with a disclaimer: The names of all those who helped me may or may not refer to real people. Further, any resemblance to real people may or may not be intentional.

I am grateful to those who expired in a timely way to

accommodate my attending funerals and for the forbearance of both undertakers and relatives; Rob and Victoria Heyland for blowing in to a great part of Ireland, and their dog Billie; everyone on the Dingle Peninsula who are too numerous to mention, but especially Sam, Lone, Antonio, Ursula, Chris and Helen O'Riordan; all those I worked with in the past and especially those who made my life in the office an interesting misery – you know who you are; Janice Gaffey for the wedding and for being cool; Austin O'Carroll, Declan Sheerin and their patients for the medical insights; everyone at Mountjoy St Family Practice and special thanks to Elaine; Phil Cahill, and Richie and his crew for the building; everyone in Ireland who still drinks in our pubs and smokes outside; my long-suffering relatives and in-laws for Christmas; Paschal, John and Ray for the politics; all those who are too cool to mention and all those who are mad into GAA. Thanks to Piotr Sadowski, Mark, Chiara, David, Steve, Catherine, Emma and Garret.

Special thanks to my editor Elizabeth Brennan for her consistent support and apposite suggestions.

For Mairead

Contents

1. Death: Is It too Hot to Bury Him
   in this Jumper? 1

2. In the Pub: Whose Round Is It Anyway? 19

3. Blow-Ins: Dingle, the Poor Plastic
   Paddy's Schull 37

4. Marriage: Even the Gluten-Free People Had
   a Good Time 63

5. Health: Overheard in the Waiting Room 87

6. Business: Enough Cheek for Two Arses 111

7. Building: Have You Seen My Tec-7? 137

8. Christmas: Who's Doing the Washing-Up? 161

9. Politics: She Doesn't Have the Hair for
   High Office 183

10. Being Cool: Bono Who? 211

Glossary 233

1

Death: Is It too Hot to Bury Him in this Jumper?

I could murder a pint.

(Common Irish saying)

Death and dying have been popular topics for anthropology since the origins of the discipline in the nineteenth century. The study of death can pose unique research challenges. On the one hand, anthropologists can become ghoulish from attending funerals. On the other hand, the anthropologist should not give the impression that funeral research is actually enjoyable. The anthropologist has a lot in common with most elderly Irish people, for whom attending funerals is an important recreation. Many of our senior citizens are delighted to have outlived their friends and go to funerals to high-five each other about the fact that it is not their turn yet. This funereal satisfaction is the Irish version of *schadenfreude*. For the anthropologist, the best research attitude lies somewhere between the imperturbable visage of the undertaker and the irrepressible grin of the major inheritor.

Behaving with élan at a wake is the hallmark of Irishness. In order to be comfortably Irish, you should learn the rules of attending funerals and, ultimately, the rules of dying an Irish death. If it is your own funeral you are attending, just lie still and look dignified. Whatever anyone says about you, don't sit up in the coffin and roar abuse at them.

* * *

Funereal Rules

Traditionally in Ireland, we used to live amongst the dead, laying them out in our kitchens after death and burying them in hillside graveyards that overlooked our towns or villages. Because their resting place was visible from the town, they could be remembered by the living. Also, from their vantage point, the dead could follow the entire goings on of the living locals. The dead also contrived to live amongst us by haunting our houses and dark roads at night.

In more recent times, we have had less interest in the dead. We have sent them to nice funeral homes or, more precisely, if they are dead pretentious relatives, funeral parlours. These parlours are homes away from home, or motels, for our dead. Nowadays, cremation is acceptable but we tend not to leave the ashes on the mantelpiece at home. However, there is evidence of a small reversal in this trend of excluding the dead from our lives with a revival of the home wake. Maybe our departed will resume their habit of haunting us in gratitude for being allowed back into our houses.

The standard Irish funeral should take place at home. Traditionally, the deceased was laid out on the kitchen door supported on four chairs.[2] However, nowadays the kitchen

---

[2] I don't know the origins of this practice, but I assume it had something to do with leaving the kitchen table free for grub at the wake. There is the related tale of the auld lad who is lying on his

door doesn't need to be removed and you are allowed a coffin. You can even be buried in a wicker basket. How cool is that?

The Rules of Dying

As a general Irish medical principle, no matter how dead you may feel, you are not dead in Ireland until your death notice appears in the *Irish Independent* newspaper. Even if you have witnessed a death firsthand, you should await the publication of the notice in the *Indo* before being absolutely certain. If you have hired an assassin to kill a rich relative, you should not hand over the final instalment of the fee until you read in the *Indo* that your relative has died 'unexpectedly'. In short, you are not dead until the *Indo* says you are.

Deaths are reported in the *Indo* according to a very strict convention. A limited number of interchangeable euphemisms are predictably used to cover the inconveniently unpredictable and unlimited modes of expiring.

The most popular way of dying, as provided by the *Indo*, is *peacefully*. This usually occurs in a hospital or a nursing home following a long illness bravely borne. Someone may also die *peacefully* at home. If you are posh it will more likely occur in your residence. *Peacefully* also covers deaths involving screaming that you don't want to go; clinging desperately to the bed-end shouting that you are still alive as they drag you away towards the morgue; throwing yourself through the hospital window to end the agony; begging for drugs to numb the pain; and running two miles down the street in a flapping hospital gown desperately seeking help from passing strangers who ignore you.

---

death-bed when he smells something delicious cooking downstairs in the kitchen. 'Is that ham?' he asks his wife, licking his lips. 'It is,' she confirms. 'But you can't have any. It's for your wake.'

As an Irish person, you can also die *unexpectedly*. *Unexpectedly*, unlike *peacefully*, is where you go without having given any indication in advance that you were on the way out. In order to titillate the curiosity of the general reader, the phrase 'following a tragic accident' is allowed in conjunction with this description. You can also use the phrase 'after a short illness', which is used in the case of a botched operation. 'After a long illness', which can be used in conjunction with *peacefully*, is used in the case of a several botched operations in a row. *Unexpectedly* does not cover: fell out of tree while cutting the branch on which they were sitting; fell off the roof while adjusting the satellite dish; blown up while faking own suicide because they sparked up a fag while forgetting that the house was filling up with gas; spontaneous combustion; assassination; by appointment with a cannibal dentist; all of the above combined. These fall under the term *suddenly*. Irish people die *suddenly* by being hit by a meteor; assassination by an impatient relative; or choking on vomit after a drunken rampage. Both *suddenly* and *peacefully* sometimes appear in parenthesis, which emphasises their euphemistic meaning, indicating to the reader that a lurid imagining is permissible in this case.

To appreciate the subtle difference between *suddenly* and *unexpectedly*, think of your rich relations: a relative can die *unexpectedly* before you have had a chance to persuade them to include you in their will; they can die *suddenly* after they have agreed to make you a beneficiary. The subtle difference between *peacefully* and *unexpectedly* usually involves a passive or active medical intervention: the *peacefully* deceased may have throttled the doctor to get their hands on a lethal dose of painkillers, while the relatives may suspect that the doctor throttled the *unexpectedly* deceased to shut him up. Whether the death is described as peaceful or unexpected is a matter of family interpretation.

In the *Indo* notice it is also *de rigueur* to mention that the death is deeply regretted by the surviving family and relatives, in case there is the least doubt in the mind of the reader. The rules of death notices demand that we promote an untypical politeness free from any sordid detail. This is the opposite of what we do ordinarily.

You are not going to learn from the newspaper the details of what actually happened. If you want to know that, you have to attend the funeral to get the gossip. That is why you need the details of the funeral arrangements, which are helpfully included in the death notice. At this stage in the process, you know from the paper both the identity of the deceased and that they are actually dead. You know you have to attend the funeral to find out exactly what happened. But before that you have to work out how much attending is going to cost you.

A Costly Death

If you are going to die in Ireland, and you have Irish friends and relatives living abroad, you should try to die during a flight sale because Irish people are reluctant to fly anywhere except at rock-bottom prices. Budget airlines are no longer enough; we want a sale. If you don't die during a flight sale, don't expect to see anyone from abroad at your funeral.

A traditional way of starting a conversation in Ireland is to ask the person beside you to have a guess. It can be a guess about anything: 'Guess how long I have this coat,' 'Guess how much the barber charged me for this haircut' or 'Guess what I am thinking now' are all popular guesses. If you do fly into Ireland for a funeral, you should participate in this guessing tradition by asking your fellow mourners to guess the price of your flight. In the graveyard, overcome any awkward moments with this game, in which as many players as you like can participate. The game goes like this: Player A (who starts) says: 'Guess how much I paid to fly in here from Chicago, return. I'll give you a clue. The taxi from the airport cost me more than the flight.' Player A should now laugh smugly. Player B should try to guess something reasonable but cheapish. He shouldn't guess one cent, for example. That would be a breach of the rules. Player B says: 'Oh, I don't know. Two hundred euro, return.' Player C now joins in by under-guessing Player B: 'One hundred and fifty.' Player D: 'One hundred and ten', etc. Player A should stop the game before the guessing becomes accurately low, at which stage it may involve up to twenty mourners. Player A now responds with the answer: 'Will you feck off with your two hundred euro.' He should grin with conceited satisfaction. 'Four euro, seventy-five cents.' Pause for effect. 'Return.' Pause for more effect. 'With bags.' At this point, the mother of the deceased says: 'Will you please shut up and show some respect while the coffin is being lowered.'

Mourning Status

As in the world of show business, with its convenient celebrity status listings, it is helpful to divide the mourners at a funeral into categorically distinct groups using the same alphabetic system favoured by the stars. A-list mourners are those who are genuinely bereaved. They include the spouse or lover, siblings, parents, children and real friends, who are devastated by their loss to the extent that they cannot really enjoy the funeral per se. Obviously no one wants to be an A-list mourner because grief gets in the way of what is otherwise a very social occasion.

For the purpose of detailing the rules governing attending funerals, I am only concerned with B-list mourners and below. You can qualify as a B-list mourner where, for example, the deceased was a seldom-seen relative, an in-law you didn't like, or an aunt or uncle from whom you have reasonable hope of a small legacy. A-listers who have inherited very large amounts of money from close relatives may qualify as B-list mourners because they may enjoy the event despite appearances. C-list mourners are those in attendance at the funeral of a relative of a friend or those at their boss's funeral. D-list mourners include distant relatives, friends of friends and those mourning a newly discovered distant cousin who died while those D-listers were in Ireland on holiday. D-listers also include the elderly who are happily burying each other as a day out of the house. As a general rule, the further down the alphabet you are, the more likely you are to enjoy the funeral.

The Travel and Dress Rules

It is not necessary for C-list and lower mourners to travel long distances to attend funerals. One's connection with the deceased should be carefully calculated against the distance to the funeral. Funeral attendance etiquette demands that A-list mourners must travel any distance, while hangers-on and funeral groupies should confine themselves to within a distance of twenty kilometres to the grave. Anything above that will appear as social desperation and probably qualifies as perverse.

When considering the appropriate distance to travel for a funeral, it is also worth considering the dress code. Low-grade mourners should ideally wear dark colours such as navy and brown, but not black. Only the A-list mourners should wear black ties. Bright colours and cocktail dresses along with feather boas and fascinators should also be avoided. While funerals can be enjoyable occasions, it is important to maintain the proper façade of respectful seriousness until at least the after-burial drinking session, where you are allowed to laugh out loud.

Similarly, when it comes to the expression of grief, B-listers and below should be careful to mourn at the precise appropriate level. B-listers flinging themselves into graves after the coffin in inconsolable grief will only give rise to speculation or gossip.

Divorce in Irish society has produced the complication of whether the ex-spouse or the current spouse can claim to be the main mourner. It is not unheard of for fights to break out as to who is the most bereaved. Remember, in theory there is no limit to the permissible number of A-list mourners allowed to fight with each other at your funeral.

Funeral Stages

Depending on your mourning status, there are different stages of the funeral you may be obliged to attend. The first stage is where the corpse *reposes* or is laid out. The deceased reposes in one of three locations. They may be put on show in a funeral home if they are relatively poor and have a small or unattractively furnished house; in a funeral parlour if the deceased is equally poor but has social aspirations; or in their own home, or residence if they don't have a home, if they are either well-off or bohemian and don't care about their furniture. It is permissible to openly enjoy the repose as a B-lister and below.

The second stage, following repose, is where the body is moved to a church in a ceremony called the *removal*. This happens even in the case of strident atheists who have left strict instructions not to be removed to a church. In contemporary Ireland there are humanistic funerals, but I was unable to find one for the purposes of this research. However, I have attended the removal of a Jewish corpse to a Catholic church.

Finally, there is the burial itself, which involves the funeral proceeding to the graveyard or crematorium where the body is buried or burned. We are even promised the possibility of having eco-friendly burials in the near future.

Each of these three formal stages involves a variety of forms of socialising. It is acceptable to attend one, two or all three parts, depending on your status as mourner. B- and C-list mourners may choose to attend both the repose and the evening removal of the remains to the church the night before the burial, or they may only attend the burial itself and the reception afterwards. D-listers and lower hangers-on generally attend all parts of the funeral without any self-consciousness or shame.

Reposing Rules

For research, I travelled to West Cork to attend the funeral of a distant relative as a B-list mourner. By normal convention I should have attended as a C-lister, but I boosted myself up one notch for the sake of anthropology. In normal circumstances, I might not have bothered because of the distance and poor roads, but the responsibilities of ethnographic research got the better of me.

The deceased, Joe-Pat, was a farmer who had accumulated a fine spread of grassland over the five decades of his farming career. He was the youngest of four siblings, with three unmarried sisters. He had also never married. All four lived together harem-like in the farmhouse and each of the sisters actively competed for their brother's affection. Platonic, of course. I remember the domestic scene from the rare occasions on which I visited. Each sister would rise earlier and earlier in the morning in order to be the one who made him his morning cup of tea. Those who were beaten to the breakfast would travel to the nearby town to select some titbits to enhance his lunchtime meal or a small gift of socks or underwear that would be preheated on the radiator before being allowed to warm the appropriate extremity. While he was a hard-working farmer, the sisterly rivalry had turned him into a domestic incompetent.

Joe-Pat had built a big house for the four of them on top of a hill for the specific purposes of being able to see his land from all his windows and – just as important – to be seen. In some countries farmers hide themselves and their houses behind hills and screens of trees to shelter from the wind and weather. Those farmers are invariably modest minded and unassuming but ultimately anti-social, because anyone lost or needing help will not know where to find them. My cousin liked to be seen. While immodest and pretentious, he was also social and generous to strangers who could easily find the highly illuminated hilltop house if lost or needing cups of tea. In the words of one of his neighbours, 'He was that kind of man you wouldn't know what kind of man he was, if you know what I mean?'

The *hacienda* is the architectural template for many vernacular farmhouses built in Ireland since the 1970s. The Southfork ranch, in the television series *Dallas*, has also provided design inspiration. Both these influences are present in my cousin's farmhouse. A narrow road winds around the hill up to the house, which only comes fully into view at the very last bend. Driving up to the house at 11.00 a.m., I saw my dead cousin in an upright coffin, plainly visible through the sitting-room window, enjoying a final inspection of both his land and the mourners coming to view him in repose.

I had dressed in discreet grey for my posing as a B-list mourner. The instant I stepped through the front door, I was handed a glass of whisky, a thick slice of tipsy cake and a turkey sandwich. The repose was well underway.

The Never-Speak-Ill-of-the-Dead Rule

When first confronting the corpse laid out on a bed or on the kitchen door or, in this instance, standing up in a coffin by the window, it is important to be complimentary about its appearance. This rule of complimenting the corpse is part of the general rule that you should never speak ill of the dead, no matter how public or notorious their shortcomings. Helpfully, in the context of commenting on a corpse's appearance, there is a range of standard expressions. These, no matter how seemingly incongruous, may well be true. This is their virtue. They include: 'He has never looked better a day in his life'; 'He is the picture of health'; 'She looks like she is sleeping'; 'You wouldn't know there was anything the matter with her'; 'I had no idea he was such a handsome man.' Frankness and honesty in general are definitely not called for. Expressions such as 'He won't be bothered by that unsightly growth now', 'I didn't realise he was so wrinkly up-close' and 'How much did you say he left you?' should not be used even when drunk at a later stage of the funeral.

Once you have complimented the corpse you can move on to enquiring about the circumstances of the death. It is customary to enquire in a general way with the question 'What in God's name happened?' A general enquiry should lead to a detailed description of the death, involving X-rays, where available; an hour-by-hour diary of the final day with all of the who-said-what-to-whom; and detailed medical notes. In my cousin's case, I already knew that he had, according to the *Indo*, died peacefully in his sleep, but I was naturally curious about the details. As it happened, he had fallen from the barn roof, while nailing down sheets of corrugated iron in a high wind, just two days after getting home from hospital where he had a heart bypass operation. He had indeed passed away peacefully, following two weeks in a vegetative coma. His sisters had argued bitterly amongst each other about which one of them would turn off the life-support machine. When they agreed it would be murder, they fought to avoid the responsibility. When they were subsequently persuaded that it would be a mercy, they fought with each other for the privilege.

Once the circumstances of death are established, you can move on to general conversation. It is customary to avoid discussing your positive future plans, the meaning of life or anything to do with being alive in general. Standing in front of the corpse is not a good place to hold forth on novel existential insights into the meaning of life, nor is it an occasion to query the value of the life just completed by the deceased. If you have a view on his eternal damnation, you should keep it to yourself. Saying, as one drunken mourner said of his dead neighbour, 'I am not surprised that he looks a bit hot now' is socially inappropriate. Your choice of conversation should be suitably glib or innocuous. As a general rule, in the Irish context, the more profoundly life-changing the occasion, the more innocuous the observation required. The stupefied silence of the traumatised witnesses to a major disaster can be overcome by the suggestion that you put on the kettle and make a cup of tea.

When I arrived, my cousins, the sisters, were in the process of reproaching each other about whose fault it was that their brother was on the barn roof during a storm. Each volunteered that they should have ascended the rounded roof of the barn to nail down the loose iron sheets herself. Each said that she would gladly take her brother's place in the vertical coffin if she could: 'I would be gone now, but he would still be here with his remaining sisters'; 'He is the greater loss.' It is essential not to attribute blame to any of the principal mourners at a funeral by actively agreeing with these superficial utterances. While you can think what you like, you should never give your thoughts voice. Stick with broad observations: 'Didn't he go peacefully in the end?', 'marvellous age', 'great life' and 'better to go while still independent' are all acceptable mutterings while viewing the body in repose. These expressions can be thrown into any part of a conversation with an A-list mourner, whether you are drunk or actually still sober. Asking for copies of biopsy reports and an exact time-line of the so-called accident or actually voicing your suspicions of foul play can wait until you meet the D-listers drinking in the kitchen.

A group will usually sit around the coffin to help you along with these awkward mumblings, and you can join them when you have completed your formal viewing of the body. Alternatively, you can retreat to the kitchen, find a quiet corner in which to hide, and drink with the D-listers. When not hiding in the kitchen, hangers-on should occupy the most visible perches. It is acceptable for B-list mourners to commence drinking and eating almost immediately. Loud laughter should be delayed for as long as possible. When it does break out, it should be confined to fellow B-listers and below.

The D-list mourners in the kitchen at my cousin's wake informed me that I had missed a row that broke out amongst the sisters over how their brother should be dressed in his coffin. One sister had insisted that he wear a favourite light blue woollen v-neck jumper under his suit, while another sister insisted that he would roast in that, as it was one of the warmest autumns in years. 'I suppose it depends on which way he's going: up or down,' one D-lister observed.

It is important for social harmony at a funeral to identify and hang out with your own level of mourner and below if you are not on the A-list. Ideally, you are allowed to social-ise down the mourning league but not up. Lower level mourners should only speak to higher-level mourners when addressed by them. Fellow guests will quickly try to estab-lish your mourning status by asking you directly how you know the deceased. They might ask, 'Who are you, now?' or 'What connection do you have with Joe-Pat?'

It is common for a number of mourning siblings not be on speaking terms with either each other or the deceased. This silence often dates back to unsuitable youthful marriages or, more commonly, land-based disputes. However, once a sibling you have not spoken to for twenty or more years dies, you should feel free to attend the funeral as the most grief-stricken A-list mourner. Cry and wail with everything you have. You should remember the don't-speak-ill-of-the-dead rule and confine yourself to only positive anecdotes on the life and times of the deceased.

Funeral Food Rules

While alcohol is a vital social lubricant at Irish funerals, food also plays an important role. If you are unable to drink because you are a designated driver, you are permitted to become obsessed with the food. When someone dies, particularly in rural areas, the neighbours bring offerings of food to the house of the deceased. These donations should be traditional Irish dishes or at least recognised as being traditional, considering there is very little variety in vernacular cooking. The food should be conservative and not draw attention to itself or boast of any culinary accomplishments on the part of the cooks. Do not bring ethnic or nouvelle cooking to a wake unless you are an established artist with an international reputation. Standard conservative cooking to suit the occasion includes roasted meats of any domesticated animal. Hare, rabbit and wild fowls, including pigeons, are not acceptable. Beef, lamb, turkey and chicken are all acceptable if overcooked. Chicken can often appear undercooked, adding to the general awareness of the fragility of life that can dominate our thinking at funerals. Ham is a mainstay but not in carbonara. Duck a l'orange is also out. In fact, forget about duck in general. Curry, if mild, is okay, while white-bread sandwiches and cakes are particularly welcome. Any form of dessert generously smothered in whipped cream will not invite negative comment.

Standard reposing, or waking, activities include singing, crying, card playing and storytelling. At one wake I attended, the traditional ghost stories were replaced by accounts of alien abductions of neighbouring farmers and a traffic accident involving a flying saucer that was reported to the local Gardaí, so it must be true. Aliens are abducting an alarming number of farmers across Ireland.

Removal Rules

The next day, it is time to put the lid on the coffin and follow the hearse to the church. Obviously, this is one of the most difficult parts of the funeral for the bereaved. In the case of Joe-Pat's sisters, I wanted to give them privacy. However, I was too slow in making my exit and found myself, with one or two other stragglers, locked into the room with the upright coffin, the undertaker, Joe-Pat and his sisters. The sisters circled the coffin, each one kissing Joe-Pat and saying her farewells. However, the first sister came round the back of the coffin and kissed Joe-Pat again, with slightly more passion, and motioned to the undertaker standing by with the lid that he should put it on *now*. Before he could move, the second sister ducked in her head and gave Joe-Pat one last kiss. Not to be outdone, the third sister kissed him again and the first sister went straight back around for round three. This circling of the coffin lasted several minutes before the undertaker dived in between the sisters, pushing them aside, and screwed on the lid, shouting, 'Enough now. That's enough kissing.'

Once the coffin is in the hearse and it is moving off, the local politicians will make an appearance. They will join the A-list mourners, sometimes walking in front of the hearse but always openly sobbing. From a sociological point of view, I assume their grief is at the loss of a voter. An ideal time to strategically join the funeral is when the cortege reaches the church and the main mourners are seated inside according to rank. Attending this part of the removal is the best way to be seen with the least input. It is customary to offer your condolences at this point. Make your way along the rows of mourners, shaking each hand and muttering, 'Sorry for your loss.' In the case of being actually sorry, you can say, 'Very sorry for your loss.' When you reach what you consider to be the C-listers, stop shaking hands.

Grave Rules

If you are an A-list mourner, you may be entitled to participate in the inevitable row that will break out over family graves. This is particularly important to older generations who have been planning their funerals for decades or to siblings who are no longer on speaking terms. A traditional form of marriage proposal was to ask your intended if she would like to be buried with your people. Surprisingly, not taking this as a threat, the woman would agree if she wanted to get married. The introduction of divorce has complicated the issue of family graves. The basic principle is that, if the plot is big enough, lifelong enemies can be buried with the more conciliatory relatives lying in between, forming a peace-line between the rival factions.

An informant told me that his distant English cousin had attended a funeral in Ireland as a C-lister. During the wake, the Irish cousins had persuaded him to carry the coffin to the grave. It is a great honour to be asked to be a pallbearer, especially if you are a C-lister. For practice, the proposed pallbearers – five Irish and one English – marched around the garden carrying the dining-room table between them. The Irish ones insisted that the tradition was to use a goose step, which they demonstrated in the rehearsal. Then the five Irish sobered up and forgot about it. The next day, however, because the English apprentice pallbearer was the only one of the six goose stepping, he inevitably fell over, knocking the coffin against a headstone and catapulting the corpse into the arms of the assembled mourners, who immediately learned that undertakers dress bodies by cutting the clothes along the back so that they can be wrapped on from the front. The naked-backed body was hastily rewrapped, relaid into the shattered coffin and gingerly lowered into the ground. The English cousin returned immediately to Coventry.

If you don't humiliate the deceased and his A-list relatives by dropping the coffin, you may be invited to the after-burial lunch.

* * *

There is a very old tradition in Ireland that, disappointingly, is no longer practised. In the past, several of the mourners would run to the home of the deceased while the rest made their way to the burial in the graveyard. At the house, they would quickly paint the outside walls, usually a dramatically different colour. This was to make sure that, when the spirit of the deceased found his way back to the house, he would fail to recognise it and wander off, thereby leaving the home free of his haunting presence.

Nowadays, after the funeral is over and the mourners have dispersed, it is not clear where the spirits of the departed go. What is clear is that, wherever they are hanging out, they read the *Indo*. This is not just to find out who may be joining their ranks but also to see if their relatives are keeping them in mind. This is why each year we write messages, usually in the form of poems, to our dead grannies and relatives in general to let them know how much we still miss them. Ideally, if you really miss them the meter and rhyming should be just slightly off. The most devoted poems are not professionally composed.

This one is for my grandfather hovering up there in heaven. Hi Granddad, I hope you like this:

Granddad, you were taken so quickly,
We hardly knew what to do.
Okay, maybe we didn't paint the house so swiftly
Because, next day, we knew it was you

When we woke to the sound of Elvis tunes,
That familiar humming and singing;
The arthritic creak of your pelvic bones
On the stairs where you're jiving and swinging;

Your unique aroma of tobacco and farts
when you bang the doors and flush the loo.
If you cease your haunting arts,
I'll write an *Indo* memorial for you.

2

In the Pub: Whose Round Is it Anyway?

The problem with some people is that when they aren't drunk, they're sober.

(William Butler Yeats)

Happily, there are no pretend 'good old days' in Ireland that we can withdraw to in our imaginations. If you are Irish, you have no opportunity for nostalgia because, as you know from your history, the future is the best of times. We have to stay firmly focussed on our possibilities.

History looks for the truth of a narrative, while anthropology recognises that meaning is often found in places other than in the company of the truth. The first principle of Irish pub life is that boring reality should be left at the door because the facts should never get in the way of a good story. Our stories help us to give our lives meaning by reinventing ourselves anew every day. The pub is the nearest we get in our culture to what anthropologists call *liminality*: being on the threshold between several states of consciousness, either psychological, metaphysical or alcoholic. Anthropologically, if you want to discover the meaning of our everyday lives, you have to go to the pub. Naturally, the appropriate research methodology is participative drinking.

* * *

The Rules for Assembling Your own Pub

We have become famous, or perhaps notorious, for our pubs. The pub is the best place to talk, and it's good to talk even when no one is listening. In fact, it is best to talk when no one is listening. In that regard, the pub is like psychoanalysis. The traditional Irish pub is now available in a self-assembly flat-pack that can be shipped all over the world. If you can't be bothered going out or you live in Nepal, why not get yourself your own Irish pub? Imagine the scene in Minsk when an eager would-be publican excitedly unpacks his boxes of pub on his bedroom floor, and organises the step-by-step instructions which are printed on the back of forty-six beer mats. These itemise the included stools, counter-tops, pint glasses, beer taps and barrels, stuffed representatives of indigenous Irish fauna, cut-out leprechauns, and fatigued-pine tables and chairs, which are the elements of the traditional pub. The directions will helpfully indicate the precise arrangements of these components to maximise *the craic* (pronounced 'the craic'), hitherto supposedly only available on the Emerald Isle itself. The craic, as explained in pub-assembly kits, is the name given to the spontaneous outbreak of unpredictable social interaction in Irish pubs. This is a bit of a swindle because back in Ireland you only use the concept of the craic if a) you are a sociologist carrying out research into Irish behaviour in pubs; b) you are drawing up self-assembly pub instructions; c) you are an historian of ideas; d) you lack spontaneity and should be at home in your own pop-up pub and not bothering people in an actual pub; or e) a group of tourists comes into a pub looking for it and you point at a stuffed badger.

But how are you supposed to know that there is no craic in a real Irish pub if you come from a place where there is no Irish Diaspora and no knowledge of Irish pub life, or even a tradition of drinking pints? Pity those from the Mediterranean, brought up on effete glasses of wine, or the Japanese, who are accustomed to shots of Sake, having to down twenty-two pints of Guinness for the sake of the craic. Our leading export success, that is the ersatz pub, is evidence of the power of the idea abroad that only we Irish know how to really enjoy ourselves. If the proper pub parts are provided, this enjoyment can be shared by anyone. But this idea is a huge marketing lie. We don't have any craic in our pubs. That is a myth created by the tourist industry.

Picture the scene: a pub packed with Irish people quietly sitting doing nothing. When a pair of tourists walk in, at a secret signal from the barman, the place erupts into an explosion of laughter, shouting and mayhem. This is true except that I am exaggerating slightly. We don't sit there silently. Before the tourists arrive we are engaging in *messing*.

Messing is to the Irish what the craic is to tourism. Messing is what we do all the time in school. 'Slattery stop messing down there at the back and get on with your work,' was a familiar reprimand from my childhood. Messing is also what you do at the back of a bus. As an Irish child, you learn messing in school as training for your later pub life. In order to know how to mess properly, it is best if you went to school in Ireland. But messing is a form of spontaneous behaviour that can conform to rules. Unfortunately, the would-be publican in Minsk is missing the instructions on how to mess in an Irish pub. He only has the ones about the craic.

How to Mess

The physical environment of the Irish pub is not its defining characteristic. Rather, it is a three-dimensional stage on which we play out the dramas of our daily lives through the social interaction we call messing. There are rules that determine one's success or failure at messing. If you meet people in the pub on a daily or weekly basis, conversation should focus on relating the events of your life during the previous day or week. The more often you meet, the greater effort is required in thinking up new things that happened to you. This is a branch of messing called *talking shite*. When you are more practised, it's called *talking pure shite*, which is one of the highest forms of messing.

Shite should be reported as if it is true and should be delivered with such frequent and blatant reference to customary techniques for demonstrating its veracity that your audience cannot but believe it. Pub conversations usually contain such phrases as 'May God strike me dead if I am lying' (lean away from the speaker for safety), 'As God is my judge', 'I am not telling you a word of a lie', 'I swear on a metre of Bibles it happened', 'To be honest …', and 'I am not lying.' In talking shite, there are no facts. The more outrageous the story, the harder you should work to make it believable. If your best rhetorical skills fail you, say, 'Right so, I can't help it if you don't believe me. There is no point talking to thick bastards like ye who think I am a liar.' Then move to the next table and see how you get on there. Talking shite is very challenging because it is the act of balancing the completely fantastical with the just credible. Alcohol will play a part in breaking down the natural resistance of your audience to shite. That is why so much alcohol is served in pubs. Remember, be prepared to stop instantly when any tourists enter the pub and start the craic immediately.

Topics for pub conversation can relate to your own relationships in the past, present and future, and the relationships of your friends, family and complete strangers that can be made interesting. It is okay to discuss politics, religion, sport, sex, the state of the country, travels past and planned, and personal traumas from home, work or college, as long as you are sure that no one is actually listening. But pub conversation etiquette does demand that when someone is talking shite, you should demonstrate you are pretending to listen to the points being made. This can be achieved through the use of a number of customary expressions of interest. These expressions allow you to think what you are going to say next while looking like you are listening. Examples of these useful Hiberno-English expressions of evidence of listening, when you are really not, along with their English translations, are:

'I don't believe you', which is 'I do believe you' in Hiberno-English.
'Go away out of that', which translates as 'Don't go away out of that.'
'Fuck off, will you' translates as 'Do not fuck off, will you.'
'God preserve us from all harm' translates as 'Nice One.'
'You're some bull-shitter' translates as 'I am nominating you for a Pulitzer Prize.'
'Christ Almighty' translates as 'Wow.'
'Jaysus Christ Almighty' translates as 'OMG.'
'That's very interesting' translates as 'You're an anorak.'
'That's pure shite' translates as 'That is very interesting. Keep going.'

These expressions are useful because it is difficult to drink, think and listen, let alone drink, think, listen and talk all at once. If under pressure, it is normal for you to cease thinking. But, helpfully, there are many guides to how much you should drink. You have drunk too much when you become boring. However, unfortunately, when drunk, it becomes impossible to recognise that you are boring. You need to nominate a trusted friend in advance to tell you. They will do this when you make the same point fourteen times in a row. You have also drunk too much if you are illustrating your shite with standard violence such as the familiar headlock or sitting on your interlocutor's face. An essential rule of pub life is knowing exactly when to go home: not too early and not too late. The memories of the night before are better when you can just remember them and when you vaguely remember 'acting the eejit' rather than 'acting the maggot'.

Pub conversation may begin with reference to actual news items or major world events and build on this foundation. These topics can form the basis for elaboration. Boasting is acceptable only as a prelude to describing self-inflicted disaster. 'My boss said I was brilliant. He gave me a promotion and a fifty per cent pay rise that brings my pay to almost three euro an hour. I was so happy I lost track of what I was doing and set fire to the building, which burned down. So we had to move to a cowshed twenty kilometres outside town.' Your respondent may say, 'Jaysus Christ Almighty' or 'Really?' Then you typically say, 'No. I'm only messing,' leaving doubt as to which part, if any, of that day's news was real. Talking about people who no one knows, particularly the opinions of people no one knows, can be boring. 'I sat beside a guy today on the bus and he told me that he was a Shamrock Rovers fan' is boring. You should add a little context to make it interesting: 'I sat beside a guy today on the bus. He told me that he kidnapped a Shamrock Rovers player, strapped a bomb to his chest and held him captive until after a major match' is not boring. The standard response in this case is: 'Really?'

'Yes, really.'

'Are you messing?'

'No, I am not. Ask Mike – he was there.'

'So what did the Shamrock Rovers fan demand?' And on you go.

One of my favourite pub stories is the following, which has the virtue of being true. Feel free to use it, inserting yourself into the action in whatever role you like. Four second-year medical students broke into the mortuary in their college in the middle of the night and stole a cadaver that had just been made ready for dissection, having spent two years immersed in formaldehyde. At home they dressed the corpse in trousers, shoes, an Irish rugby jersey, a woollen overcoat and a hat, because the weather was cold. They took it to support the Irish rugby team in a match against Scotland. The Irish team won so they took their companion, who had proved to be an excellent talisman, to the pub to celebrate. Following a mighty session in the pub, they headed off home in an old car belonging to one of them. They put their dead friend between two of them in the back seat. Driving at ten miles an hour, they had not gone very far when they were stopped by a garda. The garda put his head through the driver's open window. Shining his flashlight around the faces of the occupants, his light eventually fell on the face of the cadaver who had been dead for two years. The garda asked the inebriated driver, 'What is wrong with your man in the back of the car?'

'Ah', said the driver, 'he's had a few too many to drink. He's sleeping it off. He'll be all right. He's in good hands. We are medical students. We are taking him home to bed.'

'Get him home and pour a few cups of hot tea into him,' says the garda. Off they drove to the medical faculty where they returned their companion to the dissection room, none the worse for his adventure.

It is not important what you are drinking in the pub as long as you have an uninterrupted supply. A few of us actually like Guinness. The rest of us just pretend to like it while recommending it to tourists, for the craic. If you are a tourist visiting Ireland and you want to find a good pub, just hide your guidebook and enter the first one you find that is crowded but with just enough room to accommodate you and your party. There may be an unemployed Japanese subway shover at the door to help you squeeze inside. If you want to find a good pub, bring good friends. You are allowed to talk to strangers and you can make an auspicious start by introducing yourself in as complicated a fashion as possible, using appropriate hyperbole. For God's sake don't say, 'Hi, I'm from Chicago.' Say: 'My plane just made an emergency landing at the airport after the two wings fell off. My wife and luggage are scattered all over Longford. I thought I would never see another pint of Guinness.' Then you are in.

Smoking Rules

The ban on smoking in pubs in 2004 became the basis of new pub etiquette with a whole new form of interaction, whereby the pub population cyclically breaks into the two groups: smokers and non-smokers. Smokers must congregate on the streets outside pubs or in the specially assembled plastic annexes, hastily erected on the sides of bars, with enough air holes to meet the regulations. Non-smokers should stay inside.

When the ban was initially imposed, I travelled to a small bar in the midlands to assess its effects. Everyone said it was harsh on auld fellas who enjoyed a harmless few fags in the local. Fags are always harmless when smoked by auld fellas whose wives may have come to the view that they have lived long enough. When I arrived at my destination, I found the entire population of the small isolated bar, including the barman, standing outside the front door trying to shelter from a light shower, and all happily sucking on cigarettes. Inside, it was warm, dry and empty. On the small round tables stood the abandoned pints of stout, which were covered with beer mats to indicate that their owners would be back.

There are rules of behaviour in smoke-free pubs. Initially, both smokers and non-smokers assemble inside. If you are a smoker, you should wait until a high point is about to be reached in a non-smoker's pure shite. Then you should loudly interrupt by announcing that you have to go outside for a fag and that everyone should wait until you get back before the non-smoker proceeds to the punch line. One or two others will join you outside. Regardless of the quality of the experience in the cold and rain, you should laugh loudly on returning to the non-smokers inside, giving the impression that both the company and sublime knowledge shared outside are huge compensation for dying younger than those remaining on the prosaic inside. If you are a non-smoker, you will be asked to 'guard the drinks', which is the signal that now is a good time to talk about those smokers who have just gone outside. Talking behind people's backs is a mainstay of pub conversation. In fairness, smokers are effectively saying 'You can now talk about me' when they go outside for a cigarette. They are outside in the rain talking about those inside with their fecking pink lungs.

If you don't smoke, to maintain social contact you can take up the habit or go outside with the smokers for, say, every other cigarette. It is clingy to go outside for every cigarette. Such behaviour may attract comment behind your back. Be mindful of the fact that, in Ireland in general and in the pub in particular, a breach of social etiquette will not give rise to a comment made directly to the offending party. Such a confrontation will be avoided at almost any cost. No one will ever say that they think your behaviour is inappropriate. The strongest rebuke may take the form of your being asked to 'Cop yourself on.' This reprimand is kept for dire emergencies.

A breach of social etiquette will result in your being discussed immediately after you leave the group in which you committed the offence. For example, if you remove your knickers while standing at the bar, wipe the sweat from your brow with them and, finally, blow your nose in them, no one will pass a comment, giving the impression to any nearby tourist that we are all as cool as cucumbers about these things. However, the second you leave the room pandemonium will break out, with everyone exchanging loud exclamations of outrage, offence and incredulity. You should begin each of your exclamations with the phrase 'Did you see that?' The worst social condemnation will take place behind a person's back and out of earshot, so it is essentially punishment that can grow and develop in the offender's imagination. What people might say about us when we are absent controls our present behaviour. Most of the time it is very effective.

Round Rules

It is important not to drink on your own because that is the only unambiguous evidence of having a drinking problem in Ireland. It is best to drink with a group of friends, colleagues or complete strangers in a large circle known as a *round*. If your friends don't turn up or leave early, you can always join another round. In a round, the members take turns buying drinks for everyone else in the circle. This involves standing at the bar for long periods of time, followed by carrying back to the table (in one go) five pints, eight shorts with accompanying mixers, two large bottles of cider with accompanying glasses of ice and three glasses of wine, one white and two red. You can hold the six packets of Tayto between your teeth. No self-respecting Irish person uses a tray. Feck that!

There are five kinds of people in a round. You can choose which type you want to be. First, there is the *first-round buyer*, who is usually up first to the bar. They get things started by saying, 'Well, what is everyone having?' This type takes generosity to an extreme. Furthermore, they are likely to become violent if opposed. They are either rich or an alcoholic or both. The second kind of round member that you can be is the *round avoider*, also known as 'that tight bastard', who orders last, if at all. They hope that the other members will be comatose by the time the round gets around to them. This person will nominally offer to buy drinks in the opening round in the confidence that the violent first-round buyer will actively resist. The encounter usually goes as follows:

Mick [first-round buyer, rubbing his hands together and hovering about the seated group]: Well? What are ye all having?
Paddy [round avoider, wedged into the most inaccessible corner of the table]: Ah no, Mick. Sit down. You are always paying for the drinks. It's my turn. I'll go. [He shouldn't move even an eyebrow.]
Mick: No. No. Paddy, I'll get these. I'll get the ball rolling. You stay where you are. Don't worry yourself.
Paddy: No. I insist. It's my shout. Oh, okay. Go on so!
Mick: I'll get fifteen bags of Tayto with that because we'll need the soakage.
Mick [muttering to himself on the way to the counter]: Tight bastard.

There are several tactics that the round avoider can use. These range from claiming to have a bad back, which prevents them from standing at the bar, to having paralysed fingers, preventing them from carrying drinks or opening their wallet. In general, it is expected that the round avoider will be as imaginative as possible in order not to gratuitously offend. Finally, when they are absolutely certain that the barman has closed the bar because he has already refused drinks to several violently drunk patrons, they should loudly volunteer to buy a round. Returning empty-handed to the table, they should claim to be very depressed by the outcome and promise to buy the first drink on the next occasion.

The third type of round member is the *round partners*, also known as 'not those two again', a group of two, which, for the purposes of the round, should be identified as one. If you are a round partner, you should identify yourself from the beginning by saying, 'I'm with him or her', whereby you mean that you form a single economic unit, one of whom has left their wallet at home because the other one has the money. These round partnerships are legitimate social ties more binding than marriage. Couples become formally recognised when they come out and admit to being 'with each other' for the sake of a round. A round partner, whose other half has already bought a round, is usually allowed to skip their turn if they are not economically autonomous.

In very large rounds there may be several sub-rounds forming, or rounds within rounds. Each sub-round may contain its own first-round buyer, round partners and round avoider. In some rounds, there will be sub-rounds within sub-rounds.

The fourth round member type is called the *normal round member*, who quietly buys their round when it is their turn. There are many counties in Ireland where the normal round member is now extinct. Normal round members have been driven out by an increase in the population of a new species, the *reluctant round member*, which is related to the round avoider. The reluctant round member is more robust than the normal round member and resists as much as possible any trip to the counter, even to buy Taytos. They usually give in but only after a great deal of palaver. There was a successful television campaign against the round in general, because it can be depressing to witness so much ducking and diving on the part of the reluctant round member.

How to Cry into Your Pint

If you feel like a good cry, go to the pub and try the traditional practice of crying into your pint. If you have any nostalgia, it should be for a time when you were even more miserable than you are now. To help with your crying, there is a canon of misery literature you can bring to the pub with you. Frank McCourt has popularised the misery genre with *Angela's Ashes*. While he has a genius for hyperbole, he is not my favourite Irish misery-guts writer. His weakness is that he tries for misery. Real misery in Irish writing should come naturally. This happens on those rare occasions of genius when the writer has an innate talent for misfortune. My favourite Irish misery book is *Peig*, narrated by Peig Sayers. In this book, misery flows like a stream between the rocks of misfortune, eventually flowing into a lake of pure grief. I like *Peig* (I am probably the only person in the history of Ireland that has ever used that phrase) for several important sociological reasons. First, it was a mandatory Irish text on the Leaving Certificate syllabus. In other words, we had to read it. It was what anthropologists call a rite of passage. In anthropology we love rites of passage and *Peig* has all the features of the most tortuous. While American students were planning their prom night, we were sitting at home in the candlelight crying over a translation from the Irish that made as little sense as the original.

For those of you who are privileged not to know, *Peig* is an ethnographic account of the life of a woman, straddling the nineteenth and twentieth centuries in Kerry. In a way, she should be my role model because, in effect, she wrote the first account of how to be Irish. The high point of her book, and of her life, occurs when she throws a turnip at someone. She married, moved to the Blasket Islands where everyone around her died (she had that effect) and where most of her innumerable children blew off a cliff (my translation wasn't very reliable). The first rule of being Irish is that you have to have suffered reading *Peig* in any language. In school, affecting apathy to *Peig* was not just a badge of honour that would get you into trouble with your Irish teacher; it would also get you out of being sent to the Gaeltacht, the Irish language reservations, during the summer holidays. I also admired *Peig* because it was carefully crafted to produce incompetence in the Irish language after a mere thirteen years of reading.

Every year now I go to her grave just to dance on it (traditional style only) in revenge for the abject misery that that book caused me. Then I go to the local pub for a cry into my pint. If Peig had died young, Ireland would be a different place. We owe her our identity. Enduring *Peig* in school is the *sine non qua* of Irishness. However, following a singular and rash outbreak of liberalism within the otherwise reliably conservative Department of Education, *Peig* is now an optional book on the Irish language syllabus. Therefore, it has lost both its iconic power and its role in our cultural formation. I worry for future generations of Irish people who no longer have to read this. I asked someone currently at school if she was reading *Peig* for her Leaving Certificate Irish examination. She told me that, actually, like, she thought that *Peig* was, like, a cow, like, and that she actually wouldn't be reading it, like. I asked her if she thought that *Peig* was the biography of an actual cow. She said, 'Not a cow with, like, milk but, like, a cow cow.'

Future Leaving Certificate Irish classes will be different from those of my generation. They won't really be Irish. They won't have anything to cry about. If you have not read *Peig* at school, do not despair of becoming Irish. There are acceptable alternatives, that we allow under strict conditions, to reading that ethnography. You can nail your hand to the bar counter or beat yourself around the head with a *shillelagh*. Has reading *Peig* affected me? Of course it has. But at least it gives me something to cry about.

How to Be Normal

Whatever culture you live in, it's important to be a normal member of that society. In Ireland we all want to be normal. I overheard the following conversation between two women, who were having a few quiet pints together in the pub, which illustrates our desire to fit in. The first woman, commenting on a mutual acquaintance, said, 'It wouldn't matter to me if she were a midget as long as she tried to be a normal circus midget. I don't mean a midget in a normal circus. I mean a normal midget in a normal circus.'

After a reflective pause, the second woman responded, 'With your one I wouldn't be surprised to see her applying to Fossett's for the job of circus midget and she actually five foot eight.'

'Of course, then she would be bitching to us when she wasn't given the job,' the first concluded philosophically.

* * *

The pub is the best place to come to terms with the fact that life keeps changing in Ireland. A blow-in friend, Rob,[3] got a pure shite conversation underway in a pub in Schull with an observation on what he thought was the most important

---

[3] Rob describes himself as Anglo-Irish because he is Irish on his mother's side and Anglo on his father's. There is an entirely separate set of rules on how to be Anglo-Irish. Historically, the Anglo-Irish tended to follow the rules of how to be English in matters of culture, science, law, religion and politics. Many became senior army or naval officers in the British Empire because they were also following the rules of how to be Irish in matters of drinking, fighting and consequently dying suddenly.

change in Ireland over the last ten years. This was the fact that 'The man who was pretending to be a woman calling out bingo numbers on national television seems to have turned back into a man again. What is going on?' Could this mean that we are becoming more conventional or does it mean that transvestites are now passé amongst our bingo audience?

One of the most disappointing changes to affect pub life in Ireland is the liberalisation of closing hours. Because most pubs can now legally stay open late into the night, it is much more difficult to engage in the exciting experience of the *lock-in*.

When pubs had to legally close at eleven, it was customary to arrive at the remoter pubs at midnight so that you could be locked in with the rest of the customers. With the reform of opening hours, this practice of locking in is rare now and only occurs, if at all, as a nostalgic ritual. While most people who frequent pubs at night believe that the extension of opening hours is a good thing, from an anthropological point of view I regret the passing of an important tradition that produced a shared social bond amongst those breaking the law.

The practice of circumventing formal pub hours has a long history in Ireland. The closing of pubs on certain days and at specific hours usually only increases the desire for the unavailable drinks. It is still common to see people running around the streets in a panic on Good Friday, gasping for an illegal drink, despite their own stockpiles at home. Everyone knows that a legal drink is not the same thing. Because the pub is supposed to be closed, being locked in produces a special social bond amongst the customers not available during normal opening hours. This bond was not lessened by the fact that the practice of locking in took place every night in the same pubs at exactly the same time. The lock-in would sometimes be delayed until the last tourist had left the premises because tourists will usually 'get out now' once they have been told to do so by the barman. Once the last tourist was out, the door would be bolted, the black-out curtains drawn and the illicit drinking could begin.

In order to maintain the tension at my local lock-in, it was necessary for the Gardaí to organise sporadic raids. What is the point in breaking the law if the law doesn't ever chase you? Every three weeks or so, the barman, after peeping through the curtains at the street outside, would whisper loudly, 'Quick, take your drinks and get out the back – the Guards are outside.' We would run into the backyard and try to stay as quiet as possible but someone would always start a whispered conversation to enhance the tension. Next day, those who were locked in together would exchange knowing nods when they met each other on the street and say, 'Close one last night.'

A typical lock-in in a country pub would consist of the barman offering educational lectures on a wide range of topics to his captive audience. These lectures typically covered the subjects of thermodynamics and political ethics. The barman would hold forth at length on the relative merits and performance indicators of diesel versus petrol engines in second-hand cars, while polishing glasses. On a different evening, there could be critical assessments of the effectiveness of our local political representatives. The most important rule of being locked in was that you could not leave before anyone else because you would then become the subject of his lectures. But you could also be picked on by staying put.

One night, the barman pointed at me sitting up at the counter and, addressing his audience, said, 'Look at your man there. What kind of a fecking doctor is he? He won't treat children or animals who are a bit peaky and he calls himself a doctor!'

I tried to defend myself. 'You know our former Taoiseach Garret FitzGerald?' I said. 'He didn't treat children or sick pigs and he was a doctor.'

'Ah, I see,' said the barman, suddenly enlightened, 'You're in the fecking Fine Gael party.'

3

Blow-Ins: Dingle, the Poor Plastic Paddy's Schull

Other people have a nationality. The Irish ... have a
psychosis.

(Brendan Behan)

There are two reasons why anthropologists study cultures that are not their own. First of all, it allows the anthropologist to see what is noteworthy in a culture that may remain invisible to the native. Second, it is customary for the anthropologist to compare a culture with their own to provide insight into both. For example, nineteenth-century anthropologists were disturbed by stories of cannibalism in newly explored parts of Africa, not because of an innate vegetarianism but because it caused them to wonder if Europeans were cannibals at any time in their own cultural development. Contemporary foreigners, travelling to Ireland for the first time, might suspect that we have cannibalistic tendencies because of our Hiberno-English reference to eating each other during our everyday interactions. But the verb 'to eat' has no culinary etymology in this context. When an Irish child tells her parents, 'In school today Miss Murphy ate me because I was daydreaming in class' or someone says to you, 'She will eat you if you tell her that her arse is big in that dress,' they are using the Hiberno-English verb which, translated into English, means 'to reprimand'. Hiberno-English synonyms are the verbs 'to attack' or 'to savage'. Thus, we can see such anomalies with the help of an outside perspective.

To help us learn more about ourselves, I look at other cultures in order to get some insight into our own. However, I didn't travel abroad for this research. Instead, I studied the foreigners who have come to live here, those strange creatures who have voluntarily given up the comforts of cultural familiarity to live amongst us. I wanted to find out from them what they think makes us who we are, or, indeed, what makes them different.

Any guide to Irishness must take into account those unfortunates who want to emigrate here as a lifestyle choice or who may have relocated here against their will as part of a witness protection programme. The practical approach, if you find yourself in this position, is not to become Irish but to pretend to be Irish. We Irish will always be able to tell the difference even if you can't. While the terms *blow-in* and *Plastic Paddy* are often used interchangeably, technically those who have come here, usually against their will, and are stuck here for whatever reason are blow-ins. Those who have come here and want to stay and adopt our habits are Plastic Paddies. This latter group think they are really Irish but it is practically impossible to fake it. However, if you are a blow-in just killing time in the West or you are an earnest Plastic Paddy, you might follow the rules for becoming Irish; you might follow the example of those who have gone before you, some of whom I interviewed for my research. Like my nineteenth-century anthropological forebears, I did have to undertake some arduous travel: I had to travel to the West to find these people.

Many of my informants claimed that people are the same wherever you go. If that were true then anthropologists would be out of a job. By looking at the slight things, anthropologists see the small differences that make a real difference. At the same time, we are not very interested in the big cultural differences.

The anthropologist must also try to ignore what is already generally well known. For example, during my research, I kept hearing that we are not as organised as the Germans. Most blow-ins also tell us that we are friendly but not intimate; even the word *intimate* makes us worried that something embarrassing is going to happen.

I also found out that, if you are a little bit different in Denmark, it is easier to fit in here than at home. It's not that we are tolerant; it's that we don't mind what people who aren't related to us do. And, yes, Danish oddballs can still be a bit different over here. Also, a number of blow-ins felt they should try harder to learn Irish because it is obviously important, though no one seems to know why.

* * *

Where to Blow into

Blow-ins and Plastic Paddies are mostly found in the West of Ireland. The better-off and celebrity ones have made their spiritual capital at Schull, in West Cork. The poor and *X-Factor* runners-up ones find refuge in Dingle, in Kerry. However, isolated groups can be found as far north along the coast as Sligo and Donegal. Individual examples have been known to settle in Leitrim. Hard-core Plastic Paddies, who crave the full-on Irish experience, blow into the Gaeltacht where they are known locally in Irish as *stroinséirí* (strangers) or in Hiberno-English as *not more eejits from Germany*.

Ideally, you should blow onto about 2.4 acres of land of mixed quality with a cottage needing renovation. You should have enough room for a plastic tunnel in which unseasonal vegetables can be grown when you can get around to it. The cottage should be restored with great care with insulation values as yet unknown in our vernacular buildings. A pylon with an electricity generator should be erected just to the side of your cottage, regardless of whether or not it works, because it is really a flagpole marking your territorial head-quarters and indicating your alien status. When you place two large solar panels on the roof, you are set for the life of the Plastic Paddy. If you can't afford to buy or renovate straightaway around Schull and you don't want to move towards Dingle, you can live in a camper van, caravan or a canvas bender beside your very own ruin. You can restore your cottage bit by bit as your dole money comes through or as quickly as your parents in Berlin can be persuaded to send you the cash.

If you don't know where to settle, a camper van can be handy because you can move off quickly. Select your camp-site carefully. First impressions can be misleading, especially for the nervous travellers who are usually found in camper vans. There is a handy rule: keep away from quiet scenic places because they are not what they seem. I will relate just one experience of many that illustrates this rule. On a particularly beautiful summer evening, a Belgian family parked their van in a remote but exceptionally scenic part of West Cork, beside a church and a primary school about twenty yards down a country lane off the regional road. The car park in which they had parked is usually deserted during the summer months when the school is closed. Rob, my Anglo-Irish informant, is himself a blow-in who lives in a house on the hill overlooking the car park, with a view of the church and over the fields to the sea.[4] Rob, looking out his window, saw the Belgian registered camper van pull off the main road and come to a stop in the car park next to a little stream. That Saturday night witnessed one of the most spectacular sunsets that West Cork could produce. Rob's heart gladdened for the Belgians who were straight off the ferry from a land without such natural wonders. He thought they would have a memorable stay. He was right.

At about 1.00 a.m., a mob of local lads gathered just yards from the camper van to indulge their love of competitive 'doughnutting' on the regional road where it widened into the corner. They spent twenty minutes furiously 'laying down rubber' from the brand-new tyres on their small souped-up hot hatches with all the noise they could get out of their screaming engines. Then they suddenly vanished into the dark only to return after a half hour for another flurry. As their established doughnutting track stretched in a ten-mile circuit around the hills overlooking the car park, the noise from all the engines would fade and grow in turn in the dark. As the bend on the road just twenty yards from the camper van happens to be one of the best locations for laying down rubber, the noise was amazing. It must have suggested to the Belgians, trembling inside their fragile van, that the world as they had known it had ended with the sunset and that Mad Max had taken over. Rob told me that the boys laying down rubber 'would be the typical local lads who would do anything to help anyone, but the din in the darkness of the night would give the newly arrived a sense that they were likely to be viciously murdered at any moment.' The cars came back regularly for most of the night

---

[4] Rob argues that, technically, as an Anglo-Irish person, he is not a blow-in but has always lived here through his historical consciousness. I deal with this argument by the traditional practice of politely ignoring it.

so there was no letup for the Belgian tourists, who may well have been contemplating a move to West Cork.

When the Belgian family woke late the following morning, they discovered that their van was wedged in between one hundred and fifty randomly parked cars. It was Mass time in the church. Rob saw that the camper van curtains were jammed shut. When Mass ended, the cars all left the car park together. Rob saw the camper van departing at speed towards the ferry and the safety of Belgium – potential Plastic Paddies needlessly lost to the country. There is no evidence that anyone is paying the locals to encourage Belgian tourists to keep moving.

It is necessary, on blowing into Ireland, to give the place a chance. Where you blow in from is an important factor in social integration because different blow-ins have different baggage. I tracked down a variety of blow-ins to ask them about their own efforts to fit in and become Plastic Paddies. Regardless of from where they blew in, surprisingly few want to blow out again. Blow-ins who arrive by accident, having boarded the wrong flight, want to stay. Blow-ins who come here for love stay long after the relationship has ended or after they have actually gotten married. People who come here on holidays don't want to leave. What is wrong with these people? Don't they have any homes to go to?

Dingle, the Poor Plastic Paddy's Schull

The further west you go, the more serious the blowing-in activity and the more seriously it is to be taken. In Dublin, blow-ins are just more strangers in the city. In Kerry, many blow-ins work flat out trying to be Irish. There is a border running between West Cork and Kerry that separates the blow-ins into the well-off, early-retired businessmen and media stars centred around Schull and their lower-rent cousins, who still have to work for a living, who cluster around Dingle. I was told by Kerry-based blow-ins that the Cork ones are more advanced. The Dingle Peninsula (Corca Dhuibhne) is a Gaeltacht and reservation area where Irish culture is kept artificially alive in an open-air incubator. In winter, the locals speak Irish to each other at the back of Mass and in the pubs. In summer, they speak Hiberno-English to the tourists and the blow-ins.

I drove to Dingle over the Conor Pass to meet a variety of blow-ins. At the Pass, the sun, which was shining all the way from Dublin, vanished behind a low wet cloud that clung to the mountaintop like a comfort blanket. Inching my way through the mist, I eventually emerged after two kilometres of road and an unknown number of years of time travel into the blow-in Shangri-La beyond. I drove down the mountain-side into the gateway town of Dingle.

Would we have been forced to read *Peig* in school if she had had a great time growing up in Dingle? Would we have had to read her miserable life story if she had been great craic? Would she have been mandatory reading if she had died young from a drug overdose which was part of a rock-and-roll lifestyle on the Blasket Islands? We would not! Her biography would probably have been banned if it had been fun. Fortunately for Peig she had a completely miserable time so we all got to read about it.

You might find Peig's relation, the local leprechaun, behind the counter in The Craic Shop in Dingle selling folk CDs and sterling silver shamrocks. He is working in the Kerry tourist industry. But, as it was still winter when I arrived, The Craic Shop was closed and a sign on the door said: 'Elfin has left the Building.' This is beside the Chowder Café. Up the hill in the direction of the church is Finn McCool's Surf Shop. Outside Dick Mack's pub there are limestone stars embedded in the footpath commemorating former famous drinkers. Many of these are from the cast of *Ryan's Daughter* who drank here when the film was in production on the peninsula in 1970. I made a note of the names. I had to Google half of them to find out who they were. Dominating the streetscape is the Presentation Convent, which, like almost all convents in contemporary Ireland, is in end-stage decline. But for just €2 you can go inside to see the magnificent Harry Clarke stained glass windows. It is obvious from these windows that Harry wasn't all that good at being miserable. He is not really an Irish artist because there is no Patrick amongst the saints. I continued up the hill as far as Curran's pub and shop where Peig once worked. I wanted to see those shelves that were stocked by the very hands of our national icon of misery.

Inside, I ordered a pint. Before I could sit down I met my first blow-in. He was an Englishman who came to Dingle as a sparks[5] on the set of *Ryan's Daughter* and stayed. He had dropped into Curran's on his way back from the funeral of a chippie[6] who had come over with him and stayed till the end. This was the beginning of my wanderings around the parish of Corca Dhuibhne, tracking down blow-ins in their traditional cottages and converted barns to find out from them the rules of fitting in. Blow-ins I spoke to on the

---

[5] When you learn how to survive an experience with an Irish builder (see Chapter 7), you will discover that a sparks is an electrician.

[6] A chippie is a carpenter when referring to a person (without reference to gender) who works with wood. A chippie is also English slang for the Irish slang term 'hoor', which is used when referring to an Irish prostitute or a woman you don't particularly admire. But hoor can also be used as a term of admiration for a successful Irish man, as in the phrase 'That cute hoor got away with it again', where the term 'cute' is used to describe his mental cunning and not his physical appearance. To avoid confusion, you should never use the term cute with reference to a prostitute. When you are an expert in these slang terms, you can say, 'That cute hoor was out with that hoor again last night' and everyone will know what you mean.

phone were comfortable with the local sat-nav technology. I followed instructions such as 'first right past the Black Cat, tenth house on the left. If you lose count, there is a red shed in the garden. I have washing on the line. A bright red dress.'

The Rules of Greeting

Blow-ins are initially impressed with our friendliness. In Ireland you can smile at strangers without arousing suspicion. One of my European informants told me that, when she first arrived in Kerry, she moved into a cottage in a tiny village. She was very impressed, if a little worried, when the locals passing by smiled at her while blessing themselves as she came in and out of her cottage. She thought that perhaps they imagined she was a benign vampire or a retired anti-Christ. It took several months for her to realise that, as she lived beside the church, they were just blessing themselves every time they passed the steeple and, of course, smiling at her – an example of local multitasking.

Apart from smiling, we also appear to be friendly because we ask them how they are when we see them passing on the street or cycling by on a wildflower-collecting spree. Committing their first social *faux pas*, they stop to tell us precisely how they are at that moment in time. Soon they learn that this is a common Hiberno-English greeting, which means 'Hello. Don't stop. I don't really want to talk to you. Keep cycling. Just shout "I'm fine, thanks" at me and keep moving.' Many European blow-ins pride themselves on their exceptional standard of English, not to mention the English and American blow-ins' competence in the language. Imagine their shock when they realise no one in Kerry speaks English. Realising their linguistic confusion, many blow-ins are motivated to start attending Irish classes in the mistaken view that the locals may be addressing them in Irish. Irish classes are just a front for Hiberno-English classes. They keep up these classes for an average of three weeks, which is how long it takes them to learn the standard responses to greetings in Hiberno-English. Here is a sample of what they learn on the syllabus:

Greeting: 'How are you?'
Response: 'Fine, thanks. How are you?' [Keep moving.]

If you are unable to move because you have been paralysed from the waist down, having been knocked off your bike by a passing tractor, you might add the traditional response: 'I'm fine. Not a bother on me. It's a grand day, thank God.' The latter idiom can be added regardless of actual weather conditions.

After meaningful social contact has eventually been established, blow-ins must learn the traditional leave-taking phrases or risk being stuck in someone's company forever. A blow-in should not say 'Goodbye' but should use the Hiberno-English expression 'We must get together soon. You must call round for tea,' which in English means 'We must not get together soon. I will die of shock and consternation if you call to my house for tea. I don't even have a tea bag.'

In the area of greeting, Continental blow-ins have made an impact on local practice: when meeting and leave-taking you are allowed to kiss the air once over each cheek. That's twice in total. Hesitation between kisses is common because this practice is new to the locals. As a local, you should hold the other in an awkward embrace while hoping they know the correct number of kisses. The new tradition is two kisses, but don't make lip contact with the skin. No one, not even the mountain men in town for the market twice a year, shakes hands. That is so passé.

The Shoes-on-or-off Rule

Blow-ins will do almost anything to fit in. Local habits that present fundamental cultural challenges just have to be endured if the population cannot be reformed. One such habit is the wearing of shoes inside. Many European blow-ins come from homes with polished wooden floors. They bring the practice of removing their shoes at the door with them to Ireland. One of my informants told me that, having settled into her new home outside Ballyferriter, she had a beautiful wooden floor installed. Every day, she liked to compulsively polish it to a gleaming shine that reminded her of the floors in her parents' house in Denmark. She was delighted that she actually managed to get people to call to her house for dinner. Imagine her terror when her Irish guests arrived at her door straight from the fields, with mud-covered boots. Staring at their feet in horror and seeing their obvious readiness to dash inside her house, she hesitated at the open door. She realised in that instant that shoe removal was not an Irish custom. The first guest pushed past her outstretched arm to begin trailing mud across the hall. In desperation she cried, 'Oh, can you please remove your muddy boots?' The boot-wearer would have been less shocked if she had asked him to remove all his clothes. He loudly wondered what kind of a foreign harlot was after moving into the neighbourhood. To a local, 'Please remove your shoes' is the equivalent of a request to strip naked before coming in. Once your shoes are off, why stop there?

For months she gave up trying to get her guests to strip off their shoes. She felt constant floor washing was a small price to pay for social integration. But one night there was an unexpected breakthrough that gave her hope. A dinner guest shyly asked if anyone minded if she removed her shoes because her feet were 'killing her'. What followed was an embarrassed fumble under the table and the naked feet were kept well hidden from the rest of the guests. But this was progress. There wasn't even an overwhelming smell.

My informant offered our attitude to feet in the Gaeltacht as proof that we have no confidence with naked limbs. We will condescend to remove our shoes only if we have a good strong pair of knitted socks on. My informant wondered if we keep our boots on because we are always ready to run out of the house if the need arises.

Continentals are better with nudity than us Irish. They will casually strut through the house without a stitch on their feet. They think nothing of taking on and off their shoes and socks in broad daylight in front of anyone. On our beaches we can be seen fumbling under large towels clamped under our chins, trying to maintain our modesty as we get our socks on and off. There are parks in Germany where Germans lie naked in the summer sun being stared at by Irish sightseers in woollen topcoats and boots.

Food and Drink Rules

My blow-in informants 'thanked God' for sending Lidl to Dingle. Lidl actually sells rye bread and goat cheese, which are the staple foods of most blow-ins. Before it came to town, blow-ins were unhappily living on Brennan's white sliced pans and Calvita Cheese. Consequently, Lidl has become a Mecca for German and Italian blow-ins. It is a place to meet and exchange gossip. Blow-ins generally find pub life too trying because very few of them can drink fifteen pints of lager in one sitting. Lidl makes the life of the blow-in more independent.

A Sicilian sculptor blow-in, Antonio, told me that he gave up going to the pub when the smoking ban came in because all his mates kept getting up and going outside to smoke. He was left inside on his own. He tried taking up smoking but it only aggravated his asthma. He got sick so he had to quit. Now he stays at home and invites people round for food, drinks and smoking indoors. Few, if any, of the Irish ever turn up because they take him literally when he says, 'You must come round tonight for pasta'; they think they will get nothing else but pasta. When they do come around, they stand outside his kitchen window smoking cigarettes while he sits inside looking out at them. Uncharacteristically for me, because I don't like to interfere with the balance of nature, I did meddle by recommending Hiberno-English language lessons to help improve his social life.

Rules for Making Commitments

Many of my blow-in informants were of the view that the local Irish are commitment phobes. In order to renege on commitments, one must first enter into them. The more commitments you can take on, the more phobic you can be when it comes to showing up. This has given rise to the local custom of undertaking to meet people at every possible occasion. Instead of talking about the weather, you should make a commitment and instantly forget you have done so. The first month of every blow-in's new life in the West is spent waiting in vain for the locals to show up for tea, coffee, cake, haircuts, hypnotherapy or even dinner.

Most blow-ins told me that, to survive, they had to radically adjust their internal clocks. They had to slow down. Those coming from big cities had to learn 'to take it feckin' easy'. This meant that, if something was scheduled to happen on Wednesday morning, it would be Friday week before anything actually happened. We are all familiar with our service providers or deliverers ringing us up demanding that we make ourselves available because they will call to our house between ten in the morning and one in the afternoon, which means five minutes to one, if at all. For blow-ins in Dingle, a Wednesday appointment with a courier or tradesperson between ten and one means a ten-day wait in the house. Everyone else promises to call for tea but never do. But if you wait long enough, perhaps fifty years, they may. The average blow-in is resilient.

One blow-in, who ordered regular supplies online for his home-based business, was told by the courier that he didn't like delivering stuff to his house and that, instead, he would leave my informant's parcels with Seamus in the vegetable shop in the village. Every couple of days, he travelled to the village and pretended to check the freshness of Seamus's vegetables, none of which he bought because they were twice the price of the vegetables in Lidl, while he casually enquired if his parcels had arrived.

Know Your Power Lines

If you ask an average Irish person about power lines, they will probably tell you that they are writing to the ESB to complain about the one running behind their house, because they are confidently expecting that either themselves or their children will grow an extra head due to the electromagnetic waves bouncing through their sitting-room. If you ask your average blow-in about power lines, they will hand you a book that either they or their neighbouring blow-in has written on the subject. Many blow-ins are attracted to the West of Ireland because of the ancient monuments, passage tombs, mound tombs and standing stones that are not randomly scattered over the landscape but built in conformity with a strict pattern of ancient subterranean occult power lines.

For the blow-in, a power line is the special energy in the landscape that marks a line connecting one ancient monument with another. The invisible lines linking our archaeological monuments are an important source of the blow-in's natural energy which they draw from the rocky geography of the West of Ireland.[7] Modern Irish people, who live in the landscape, should be aware that they are joined to their ancient rugged ancestors through these connections. The locals don't realise it, but they draw their natural energy for life from these lines. Obviously, sometimes the power is turned off. The power lines are also a valuable source of artistic inspiration for the blow-ins, the vast majority of whom are artists. Farming blow-ins live in West Cork because there are less power lines there, naturally. As it happens, Irish churches have been built on these lines without the original builders being aware of it.

Taboos

Even the most advanced Plastic Paddies do not hang out at the back of the church at Mass on a Sunday morning smoking fags with the locals. That is seen by blow-ins as a step too far. Another custom that is avoided is attending the funerals of locals, whether known or unknown. The general consensus was that funerals, in general, are too morbid. Besides, 'You would really need to know the people who are dead.' But how can you ever get to know them if you don't go to their funerals?

Continental blow-ins tend to be more comfortable with buffet food at parties, whereas we like a good feed piled in

---

[7] This energy supposedly runs underground in straight lines. Important archaeological monuments were built on the junctions because our ancestors were 'in tune' with them. Traditionally, the ESB run their power lines over ground, which makes them easier to see than their occult counterparts underground.

Don't expect me to explain what these ancient power lines are because I am not a blow-in. Blow-ins have actually written books about these energy lines and some of them don't even involve drugs. If you know what these blow-ins are talking about, you are obviously a blow-in yourself. Otherwise, just go along with it.

a pyramid on our own plate. At an Irish public feast, you should position your arms on the table to encircle your plate and mutter to yourself, 'It's mine. Keep away.' This practice probably has its origins in the nineteenth century Great Famine and is still widespread in Cork and Kerry. The buffet throws us into confusion.

Blow-ins also think it is remarkable that Irish people take longer to mature than their Continental counterparts. Parents in Denmark, for example, treat their children as independent adults on their eighteenth birthday. Irish mothers wait until their sons are fifty-three, just to be on the safe side. In Holland, allegedly, there are modern fathers who take joint responsibility for child rearing. In Dingle, there are fathers who put their children in the back of a jeep while they plough the nearby field. It's okay because they can all see each other through the windows.

Blow-ins have a lot of time on their hands. They use it to do a lot of thinking. They have developed a belief that the nearer to the sea shore you are, the friendlier the natives. On this principle, blow-ins try to congregate as near to the sea as possible. The further you go from the coast, the less friendly the people – until you eventually arrive in Athlone. The message is: stay near the sea. An historical explanation that I was given for this by Antonio was that people who lived on the coast were used to visitors who arrived in ships from over the horizon. Therefore, they are more open-minded. I thought it was a nice idea so I didn't remind him of the Vikings' reputation for making friends along the coast a thousand years ago.

Antonio's workshop is in an old forge on the coast, where the locals used to gather to exchange news and gossip over centuries, while they patiently watched their patient horses getting a new set of shoes. The horses and locals are now gone, but the anvil, furnace and stone water-trough remain. In this forge, which stands on the junction of several major power lines, Antonio makes Celtic headstones for those blow-ins that end up staying forever.

The Rules of Being the only Black Man in Corca Dhuibhne

For the sake of my anthropological investigations, I was advised to meet Sam, the only black man in Corca Dhuibhne, to find out how he became a local. I rang his wife to ask if I might meet him for a chat. She told me that we could meet in Páidí Ó Sé's pub in Ventry at half eight. 'How will I know him?' I joked. I suggested that we might wear red flowers in our lapels. She was not amused.

Ventry is a village in the parish of Corca Dhuibhne. It comprises a pub, a church, a shop and two houses. I punctually entered the huge bar, which was completely empty except for a barman behind the counter, and a white man and a black man at the bar. 'Give my informant here a pint,' said I to the barman as I shook hands with everyone. After a few minutes of me blabbing non-stop, the barman was becoming visibly irritated. I was surprised that Sam had very little English, coming from London, but he smiled and sipped his pint. 'What is your problem?' the barman eventually asked, no longer able to endure the scene across the counter. 'I am looking for Sam, the only black man in Corca Dhuibhne,' says I. 'That's not him,' says the barman. 'That's Eric, the only tourist from Paris. Arrived today.'

I sat in a far corner nursing my pint and embarrassment. After a few minutes, Eric came over to say goodbye. He gave me a crystal, thanked me in French for the pint and left with the impression that the locals were uncommonly friendly. Another black man came in a few minutes later. Going on the assumption that I had by now reached the limits of the black population of Ventry, I introduced myself again.

According to Sam, when he first arrived he was paranoid that the locals were talking about him, in front of him, in Irish. He decided to learn just the word *slán* (goodbye) in Irish. He went round to all the pubs and sat there listening to the locals talking, without being able to follow a word. When he left, he said, '*Slán.*' This caused the locals, in turn, to become paranoid that maybe he understood them after all.

Now, after more than ten years living amongst them, their jokes run to calling him a Suffolk – which is a black-faced sheep – which seemingly is hilarious if you are a local sheep farmer. They sometimes remark, 'The sun must be fierce hot over in Ventry,' and then all laugh. Sam is delighted to be included in these small witticisms at his expense because it is a mark of belonging. Laughing at an often-repeated joke is an important winter pastime, and the more stupid the joke the better.

To better fit in, he learned about Gaelic football from the television channel TG4. He learned the names of all the players on the Kerry county team going back twenty years. Kerry is handy because there is no hurling in the county. His advice to blow-ins is to slow down and practise doing everything in slow motion; practise gossiping every chance you get because this is the main pastime in the pubs and Lidl; you don't have to go to Mass if you go to the pub; get out regularly because then people won't be able talk about you behind your back. Sam told me, 'People are great around here. They leave you alone and mind their own business. If you were dead in your house three weeks they wouldn't bother you.' If you practise these techniques, you will end up like Sam.

His greatest pleasure is to come into the pub on a winter evening when all the tourists have left. He enjoys knowing everyone inside. The fire is blazing in the hearth as the rain lashes against the windows. He takes a pint over to the fire and sits down with his new family, the winter locals, for an insider's gossip and to talk shite. Perhaps a German blow-in has gone back to Berlin. They speculate about what will happen now because, when one German goes, they all go. For Sam, he is home.

Sometimes blow-ins blow out suddenly. You get up one morning, late of course. Your neighbours have either gone or are dead in their houses. You should wait the customary three weeks before checking. But before that the rumours will be flying around Lidl.

The Rules of Bending

For a balanced perspective, I worked my way along the coast in the direction of West Cork. I visited small isolated farms, small craft shops and organic food businesses on the seaboard in the direction of Schull. We owe our national identity to a small army of Plastic Paddies dedicated to keeping our traditional culture alive. Never mind your Gaeltacht; we would be lost without our blow-ins. Our *TB cheese*[8] and bodhrán-making businesses would be wiped out, along with most of our pottery and landscape painting, if they all left.

On the way I stopped in Dunmanway, which is the capital of the New Age Traveller blow-in. I visited a makeshift hippie village. The collection of semi-derelict stone cottages

---

[8] The pasteurisation of raw milk was introduced to control contagious bacterial diseases including bovine tuberculosis. Historically, TB used to be the infection of choice amongst our poets and artists but has since fallen out of fashion as a fatal disease. Apparently TB cheese tastes better than its pasteurised cousin and is definitely more exciting to eat. While raw milk products, such as TB cheese, are only legal in Ireland, they are regarded as a health food in many European countries from where the blow-ins originate. For many blow-ins, there is no better way to express their unmediated existential relationship with nature than to make TB cheese. Without their efforts, we would have only the inoffensive varieties.

surrounded a large bender that rose up like a medieval church in the middle of this improvised community. A bender is built by layering canvas or plastic sheeting across long poles that are secured in the ground at each end to form a tunnel of arches. Wigwam designs, inspired by the North American Plains Indians, also technically count as benders. The community gather in the bender for public events like meeting me. I sat amongst ten adults and their children – not to mention the dogs, cats and countless scrawny chickens – all wandering in and out of the rain, drinking tea and cider, and eating huge slices of bread that was freshly baked in a skillet, heated over ashes from the roaring central bonfire. The smoke left the bender every time someone opened the flap to get in or out.

I asked the woman who was filling the role of the wise clan elder where she was originally from and what she was doing in a bender outside Dunmanway. Like a storyteller of old, running up and down a small path beside the fire, while waving her arms and miming all the parts with great skill, she told me that she was originally from Leeds but had left her family and home when she was young in search of enlightenment as a Hindu. She travelled for years around India studying with various Brahmins, before finally queuing up at a temple to kiss the foot of a famous rishi. For an entire day and night, she stoically queued to reach the head of the massive line of devotees. Miming the part, she showed me how, at last, with trembling lips, she took the rishi's foot in her hand to plant a devout kiss on his instep as a prelude to dedicating the rest of her life to the study of the Bhagavad Gītā. Foot in hand and with puckered lips, she saw that he was wearing surgical stockings. He explained, when cross-examined by her, that he was worried about catching disease from all the devout foot kissing. She immediately dropped both the foot and her faith and, after a few more years of aimless wandering in a spiritual wasteland, she found a home in the bender in Dunmanway.

In Ireland, she explained, 'We don't wear surgical stockings. We are real!' I started to tell her about the foot inhibitions back west in Dingle but thought better of it. I was very moved by this story because it says something profound about our natural simplicity. It had nothing to do with the eight pounds of home-grown grass that they were working their way through in the suffocating bender. When I was taking my leave in traditional fashion, by insisting everyone come to visit me – 'Come for tea,' I demanded – I was surrounded and asked to stay. There was always room for one more in the bender. 'Stay with us. You can join our clan.' I pleaded that I had a clan of my own and eventually got back on my journey towards Schull.

Plasticus Schullus

The Plastic Paddies who live around Schull are of the improving kind. Their defining quality is their desire to improve us. Schull is a very improved village. Running parallel to the marina is a long street that has a tapas bar, run by real Spanish people, a fish and chip shop, run by real French people, a book shop and a venue for hosting the annual short film festival. As one rare resident, Pauline, put it, 'What more do you want?' Amongst Pauline's many roles in the village is that of taking tourists round the pubs to make sure that they are evenly distributed amongst the few locals and many blow-ins.

One of the things that makes Ireland so attractive to the blow-in, though we would be too polite to admit it, is how tolerant we all are of the noble projects to improve us that have been going on for centuries. The best way to resist a blow-in's efforts to improve you as a local is to just nod in agreement and smile. Hence the origins of our smiling and apparent friendliness, much publicised amongst blow-ins.

The improving project means that this population of blow-ins are more forthcoming about our national flaws than their Kerry cousins. Many of the Schull-based blow-ins suffer from bouts of exasperation brought on by contact with the locals, of whom there are fortunately few. Most of those live in land. But, in between these bouts, life is very harmonious. When exasperated, such blow-ins can tell us that our principal nationalistic obsession is worrying about what impression we are making on blow-ins.

Plasticus Urbanus

While waiting for the train from Cork back to Dublin, I gaped in tourist-like ignorance for any indication of which platform I should be on. I approached a friendly looking traveller.

'Excuse me. Can you tell me which is the platform for the train to Dublin?'

'Well, I am on Platform One,' she said, not so friendly after all.

'But where are you going?'

'What's that to you?'

'Never mind. I'll ask someone else.'

I was told that urban-based blow-ins are more philosophical than their country cousins. They spend more time reflecting on the meaning of Irish life. To test this theory back in Dublin, I convinced Italian friends to become my city-based blow-in informants. They are urban blow-ins but not aspiring Plastic Paddies; they are just blow-ins. She originally came to study and he followed for love. Before coming to Ireland, she was aware of some of our archaeological heritage but that knowledge was not a deciding factor; she came to study with another blow-in who was already living here and was an expert in Plastic Paddery. Her boyfriend was familiar with some traditional Irish music that he enjoyed. He had albums by Thin Lizzy, Rory Gallagher and The Pogues that made a very good impression on him and made the decision to accompany his girlfriend easier.

Ireland first struck these Mediterraneans as being disturbingly green. Almost intolerably green. They found it very hard to deal with the colour green, which eventually produced in them a Mondrian-type alienation from nature. They retreated into the brownness of the city where they have remained, afraid to venture too far into the countryside. From their first arrival in Dublin Airport, they began to notice our need to throw litter around. They have since become expert litterers. They realised that this would help them to both fit in and deal with our vivid greenness. They would advise would-be blow-ins that pocketing your waste will only draw attention to yourself.

The more observant urban blow-ins recognise that, unlike them, deep down we are very superficial – which is one of our proudest attributes. When we want to be deep, we talk about someone else's feelings. We are very friendly on the surface, which means we are actually very friendly through and through. Many blow-ins who come from more expressive Latin cultures initially suspect that we are hypocrites, because they imagine that we must have thoughts other than those we confess to having, which are the ones we express aloud, usually in pubs. This idea that we are hiding our real feelings and our true views on the world behind a hypocritical façade is a recurring view amongst blow-ins. Their suspicions are reinforced by a paranoia that no one can be as friendly as we seem to be. Friendships are made when blowins stop insisting that their new neighbours 'open-up', 'get in touch with themselves' or 'express their true feelings', and embrace our innate two-dimensionality.

In the view of my blow-in urban philosophers, we could be accused of being emotionally stunted because we give the impression that we have only a few emotions. The two most frequently used are friendliness and complaining. We give the impression that these two emotions are not linked to our circumstances at any point in time but that we access them randomly. Confusingly for blow-ins, we appear to have different feelings when we are drunk, simply because we speak louder and more emphatically. We repeat a point more than once, often very many times, in a desperate bid to win agreement from our listener on topics such as sport, where player W or team X is deemed to be the best in the world – no, really; relationships, where person Y is deemed to be a complete bollix – no, really; or work, where person Z is deemed to be a complete bollix – no, seriously.

When drunk, we have access to two less subtle emotions: sadness – or, more precisely, melancholia, which is a form of desperate complaining – and violence, which is a form of desperate protest. When drunk, we access these two emotions randomly. This makes it exciting for blow-ins to drink with locals because either emotion can suddenly appear at any point in the pub. The differences between our sober and drunken conversations cause blow-ins to imagine, foolishly, that the drunken views are in some way nearer to our 'true feelings' or more telling or profound, rather than just other superficial emotions being expressed more loudly.

Many blow-ins who come here from more sober cultures just don't understand drunken conversations because they didn't have the opportunity to practise enough when younger. The inverse of this is that, while certain blow-ins would be classified as having alcohol problems in their home countries several told me they blended in here, with their consumption of alcohol going relatively unnoticed. These blow-ins did not feel that we were hiding anything, nor did they believe that we were emotionally stunted. So there!

If you become a Plastic Paddy and convince yourself that you have mastered the rules of being Irish, you will realise with the rest of us that we are the most interesting, exciting, diverse and charming people in the world, and not at all prone to exaggeration.

* * *

I was on the no. 140 bus heading into Dublin City. Two elderly German tourists got on and put three euro each into the money slot, took their ticker-tape tickets and sat down just behind me. Out of professional curiosity, I tried to eavesdrop. They began to study their ticket printouts. From the increasingly loud German clamour, it was apparent that they had discovered that they had been credited €1.35 each, as the fare was €1.65 and no change is given on the bus. They engaged the bus driver in conversation but were twice asked to stay behind the white line and then to sit down in the interest of safety. Eventually, having arrived at their stop, they demanded to know how they could claim their refunds. The driver slowly explained that they could go to the head office on O'Connell Street. He told them that it would cost them 50 cent each to get there on another bus and that they couldn't use their current tickets. With lightning mental arithmetic, they worked out that that would leave them with a net balance of only 85 cent each. So they continued their protest and the squabble went on for several minutes. At last, a shabby, old arthritic Dublin woman slowly shuffled her way to the front of the bus. She opened her purse and took out some change. Handing some to each of the German tourists, she said: 'Listen luvs. Here's the fecking money. God help us, ye poor craters. How much is it? €2.70? There ye go.' A cheer went up from the rest of us on the bus, who were impatient to get moving again.

4

Marriage: Even the Gluten-Free People Had a Good Time

There is nothing nobler or more admirable than when two people who see eye to eye keep house as man and wife, confounding their enemies and delighting their friends.

(Homer)

Kinship studies, which are the exploration of family relationships, used to be the mainstay of anthropology. In the past, it was common for anthropologists to tour the countryside compiling charts of family members and noting the vernacular terms for the relations that we call mother, father, brothers, sisters, cousins, etc. Kinship systems throughout the world have evolved into one more-or-less standard model of what we have come to recognise as our own family structure. Therefore, anthropology has lost much of its interest in kinship studies. With a few polygamous exceptions, family structures look much the same everywhere. This is the case even if we add in gay marriage. For gay families, we just adjust the gender of the roles of mother and father or have father–father or mother–mother marriages that are passé by anthropological standards. Historically, many native American Indian families commonly featured more than one mother or father. Would you want more than one of any family member if given a choice?

But anthropology hasn't given up all interest in kinship studies because what differs from culture to culture is our various attitudes to the relationships within families. While the Irish family is similar to other Western family structures, it varies in terms of the behaviour between its members. For example, attitudes to marriage are peculiar to different cultures. Like funerals, Irish weddings provide an opportunity for social interaction. In Ireland, we don't marry for the possibility of a pleasing divorce settlement; we marry for 'a day out'.

It is obvious in Ireland that people don't get married for love. A loving couple wouldn't put each other through an Irish wedding. Why do people get married? Anthropology has not been able to provide a complete answer. However, many people do marry. If you want to be Irish, you should find yourself someone to marry and have an Irish wedding.

* * *

In the north-west of the country, marriage is referred to as a woman acquiring an extra pair of legs. Typically, someone will say, 'I see Marie is after getting herself an extra pair of legs last week,' which will be followed by a ribald guffaw. This is quite a sophisticated expression because it covers more than the standard missionary position. However, this traditional reference is outdated because nowadays it is common for most couples to live together for years before marrying. Lengthy engagements are fashionable.

Irish marriage, though not marking a significant change in a couple's relationship, is a socially formal occasion to be taken very seriously. Contemporary Irish marriages are distinguished by the difficulty we have in trying to take a casual or informal approach to the ceremony. Even eccentric couples that have their reception in McDonald's must do so with deadly seriousness.

Irish weddings are like funerals with the addition of guest lists and stress, and more opportunity to plan. Like funerals, weddings often begin suddenly, not, in this case, with a death, but with the announcement of an engagement. A number of the same principles apply. You have to determine where you are within the social pecking order and what your relationship to the main protagonists permits in terms of acceptable behaviour, presents and dress. An informant in Sligo told me: 'Funerals have weddings bate every time because there is no invitation and no present needed.'

Engagement Rules

Before a couple can announce their engagement, they should live together for so long that no one can remember a time when they were not a couple. Preferably, they should have two children with one graduated from college. Then one day, out of the blue, they should announce that they are engaged. They should plan to marry on a date yet to be determined, but not less than five years and not more than ten years from the date of this announcement, until which time the couple are to be regarded as being engaged and should be addressed as such. They should change each other's names to *my fiancé(e)* and continuously inform strangers what the other is doing and thinking at any moment in time, in case anyone might suspect that they are not actually engaged. A ring may be produced for the occasion or may be planned to be produced at a future date. An important reason for the announcement of the engagement is to test the acting skills of friends and relations who are obliged to feign delight, surprise and enthusiastic anticipation of the great day, or risk incurring the wrath of the engaged couple.

The long engagement allows the bride and groom to plan the day. It also allows the potential guests to either save up money or compose credible excuses as to why they can't attend. The contemporary *long engagement*, culminating in the meticulously planned contemporary wedding, has replaced the *short engagement*, ending in the very enjoyable and poorly planned shotgun wedding. This is an example of the unpredictable consequences of social reform – in this case the introduction of contraception. Historically, the unavailability of contraception, combined with the lack of self-restraint that characterises any banned behaviour, together with a social context where extramarital childbirth was believed to be miraculous, produced the short engagement that had an average span of three weeks. In the past, it was not unusual to receive the invitation on the day of the wedding. There is a lot to be said for reintroducing a ban on premarital sex: it gets rid of the long engagement.

In some cases, the engagement is an end in itself. One informant told me that she was 'really, really happy' because she had become engaged to 'the most amazing guy'. She was throwing a big engagement party the following Saturday night in the local pub. When I asked her when she was going to get married, she sighed and, summoning the patience she usually reserved for very stupid people, told me pityingly that she 'didn't ever want to get married'.

The Rules of Wedding Planning

The most important thing in planning your Irish wedding is that you should do whatever you can to make sure that your special day is unique. In that way, you can be reasonably confident that it will be exactly the same as everyone else's. This is an occult law of wedding planning: the extent to which you try to be different is inversely related to how similar the occasion will be to all other weddings. To reverse this trend, you could set out to be the same as everyone else and see what happens. Unfortunately for the guests, those planning the wedding never take this approach. In extreme cases a wedding planner can be hired, but the norm is to allow the bride, or more precisely her mother, to plan everything. Informal weddings should be formal. If you plan something simple, simple it may be, but it will still take years to organise.

The Guest List Rules

Once you have actually decided to get married, you must now make the more difficult decision of who will attend the wedding. There are strict conventions involved in the compiling of the guest list. This task is so challenging that many couples break up at this point, and retire to discrete parts of the house to live out separate lives.

The opening moves are easily settled. You should both agree that the wedding will be small, with just immediate family and your closest friends in attendance. That's it. Easy! According to your original calculations, this comes to a total of eleven people. You may high-five each other. Because you are both highly superstitious, after a decent interval of a few minutes, the bride-to-be should say that she couldn't have an uneven number of guests. After a good-humoured row, it may be decided that a spinster aunt be invited on her own with strict written instructions not to bring anyone with her. You agree to a contract-like form of words to be used on her invitation. On the basis of kinship alone, to counterbalance that aunt, even if she is coming on her own, two married aunts from the other side have to be invited with their husbands. This brings the proposed guest list to a manageable sixteen.

This total should be communicated to both sets of parents. A period of three weeks of complete silence – from said parents – should follow. The total ban on all communication, initiated by the father of the bride-to-be, is maintained in order to convey the depth of sulking that is actually going on. Unfortunately, this silence will be broken and there are rules for how this should be done. The mother of the bride-to-be should ring the groom-to-be after the three-week interval to announce that her husband will not be attending the wedding because 'There will be no point, really, because he won't know anyone there. Why should he pay for an event where he won't know anyone?' In other countries, teenagers sulk. In Ireland, it is fathers.

The groom-to-be, who up to this point should have maintained the naive belief that there was actually going to be only sixteen guests at his wedding, should foolishly ask which essential potential guests may have been inadvertently omitted from their original guest list. The mother of the bride-to-be should read a prepared list of family and friends over the phone. She should promise to forward a hard copy of this list in the post.

When it is delivered, the bride-to-be should have a near fatal fit. This list comes as a shock because her husband-to-be, too frightened, would not have told his wife-to-be of the phone call from his mother-in-law–to-be. By now, the bride-to-be's mother should send another copy of the list to the other set of parents under the provocative heading *Our Guest List*. This can be responded to with a counter-list of the other side's essential guests. The six should eventually agree to meet to go through the new expanded list together. Each name on the list can be identified with the help of ancient family photographs, quickly sketched family trees, copies of birth and death certificates, records of imprisonment, and stories of how 'Joe saved your father's life when a milk churn fell on him when he was a lad. Both he and his wife Betty and their two unfortunate daughters – the less said about them the better – have to be invited.' Each of the six participants should have a veto in the form of threatening not to attend the wedding in the event that a particular guest is or is not included. The veto can be used only twice by each of the fathers-in-law-to-be, three times by each of the mothers-in-law-to-be and only once by the bride-to-be. It is not appropriate for the groom-to-be to exercise his veto. Eventually, after several days in conclave, all parties can agree that only one hundred and eighteen family members will be asked, from each side.

Once the psychologically critical two-hundred mark has been passed, the couple can cave in and invite forty-six of their own friends and only twenty of their closest work-mates each. The final tally, excluding the nine priests that will be officiating, who will surely stop off for the dinner, should come to three hundred and twenty-two to be invited, of whom three hundred and twenty-nine should actually turn up on the day.

Once you have drawn up the interim list, you can then send out the invitations. There is a new DIY ethos in wedding planning in Ireland. The bride-to-be should make her own invitations or ask the groom-to-be's sister's boyfriend's cousin, who has recently started her own invitation and greeting-card design cottage industry – following a course in the National College of Art and Design – to make them for her. Alternatively, you should go early to Daintree on Camden Street, Dublin, early on a Saturday morning to avoid the hoards of couples that gather there to buy fancy paper to make their own invitations. I recommend recycled chip-bag brown paper scrolls with green Cyrillic font verse, tied up with pre-loved baling twine.

For our own wedding, my wife-to-be was in such despair about the prospect of seeing the husband of one of my relations that she requested the invitee leave him at home and bring someone with whom she could pretend she was having a discreet affair. She turned up with both.

The Rules of Worrying

All Irish brides-to-be have one thing in common: stress. One of the main causes of marriage-related stress is worrying what the new in-laws will think. Marriage would be a lot less stressful if we were allowed to marry someone in our own immediate family because at least they know what we are like, and what our parents are like, in public. However, marrying a family member is proscribed by the law of consanguinity, which is a ban on incest.[9] Therefore, we are legally forced into the stresses associated with putting our families on public display.

The best place for an anthropologist to find prospective brides for interview is in hotel lobbies where they go to book their wedding package, which is gold, silver or bronze, depending on how much choice they want to give their guests in terms of the dinner menu. I sat in hotel lobbies of the more popular wedding hotels waiting for the brides-to-be to turn up at reception. You can tell who they are because when they arrive they look significantly more miserable than any of the normal guests. They are usually accompanied by an even more worried looking older couple, who are each tightly holding an arm of the bride-to-be in case she tries to make a run for it. These turn out to be her parents. They whisper in embarrassment to the

---

[9] Most anthropologists rather lazily accept the view that the origins of the incest taboo lies in pre-historic observation that incest produces deformed off-spring. I don't believe this because it is obvious that cavemen had no knowledge of genetics. Instead, I think it owes its origins to the fact that there would be less presents at incestuous marriage ceremonies.

receptionist, like patients in an STD clinic, that they are there to see the manager about the wedding packages. Before the manager turned up to enquire about their preferred metallic entertainment, I pounced. Once the initial awkwardness had passed, they were happy to share their worries. Very stressed Irish people like to talk, usually non-stop. Okay, I admit that, in many instances, they may have thought that anthropology had something to do with psychiatry. I didn't clarify the distinction, in the interest of research. Anyway, they seemed to need the psychiatric help.

To date, no one has compiled the complete encyclopaedia of bridal worries. So here are just some of the worries that should keep the bride-to-be awake at night. If she is not awake, she is obviously not in love.

Her first worry is that perhaps she is making the second biggest mistake of her life because not marrying Shawn, her ex-fiancé, was actually the biggest!

Her next big worry is what she is going to wear. Should the dress be a Vera Wang copy or an Oscar de la Renta rip-off? At least she knows for certain that it has to be white. Her four children, not to mention her parents and Shawn, would be horrified if she went for anything other than white. What about a wrap? Does she need a wrap or will she be okay with freezing arms?

Once the bride-to-be has secured her own dress for thirty-seven thousand euro, her next worry will be how she can get the bridesmaids to pay for their own dresses, while still dictating what they should wear. The traditional practice is to suggest that, because she doesn't have the time to shop with them, they buy their own dresses and she will pay them back – at some stage. Just two weeks into the engagement, her two best friends, who are not the two who are going to be her bridesmaids, should have fallen out with her because she had to ask 'those other two' because she was a bridesmaid at their weddings. Neither bridesmaid should be talking to the other after the hen night. One of them is having a not-very-secret affair with the best man. The other has a tattoo of a snake emerging from her left armpit and a tattooed list of her exes on her right arm so it has to be long-sleeved dresses for everyone. By the time it is all over, no one will be on speaking terms until the next wedding when all details of the previous one will be forgotten.

The contemporary Irish wedding can take place in a church, registry office or under a tree but, wherever it happens, it is not a proper wedding if it doesn't have a theme. The problem with themes is that they have all been done already: Star Trek, Star Wars, butterflies, angels, hearts, vintage, shabby-chic and classic cinema. You can get away with having no theme as long as you stress on your invitations that the actual theme is *No-Theme*.

Worrying about the food should bring the bride-to-be on to worrying about what font she should print the menu in. She should decide on the Roast Haunch of Wicklow Venison with Chantenay Carrots for the meat eaters, but how is she going to cater for her friends with wheat intolerance and those with lactose intolerance with the same menu?

Another cause for worry is if the guests will know the difference between Prosecco and Champagne because the bronze package only comes with Prosecco and without the canapés.

If her budget is getting tight, she should hire just half a string quartet for the drinks reception and call it a duet. She can get the other half of the quartet to supply background noise during the dinner to drown out the sound of open-mouthed venison chewing.

Other musical anxieties include fretting about whether she should hire Irish dancers for between-course entertainment. What kind of band is she going to get? Can she afford the disco? She can because she just remembers that her friend's boyfriend is really cool and is doing a course in music at *Trinners*.[10] He has loads of equipment and he will do the disco for eighty euro. But then she should remember that he doesn't know any disco music because he is too cool. How can her parents dance to Insane Poetry?

The bride-to-be should also worry about how she can avoid inviting children. She should decide she can't avoid it because she doesn't have the nerve to tell her sister-in-law to stay at home with her three attention-seeking brats. But the children are too short to sit at the table with everyone else. They have less conversation than Aunt Louise so they will have to go in a separate corner. But should she go for a toadstool sub-theme for them? Which guests will she make sit on the toadstools with them? Should the children have miniature versions of the adult meals or just chicken nuggets? They would enjoy the nuggets but it's not about what they want. It's about what she wants. And what about what's-his-name, Aunt Mary's child, Jason, and all his allergies?

The mother of the bride-to-be may now advise her daughter that her friend's daughter got through the whole thing on diazepam. No one noticed when she eventually collapsed towards midnight after her sixth Corona. Luckily, her friend's daughter, now happily married, has a few bottles of pills left over after rehab. The mother should tell her daughter that she acquired this supply for just twenty euro because they are all friends. Those bottles and what she has herself in the bathroom cabinet should see the bride-to-be through the coming ordeal.

Who is she going to sit beside whom at the dinner? What about her uncle with the speech impediment – who is she going to put beside him? Maybe she can tell Maura that she doesn't have to buy her a present if she agrees to sit between her uncle and the deaf priest.

---

[10] Trinity College Dublin of course (see Chapter 10).

Meanwhile, the groom-to-be should worry about who will win the All-Ireland this year.

Typically, the bride-to-be should forget to order the ice-sculptures. A week after the wedding ceremony, her brother should discover a box of dead white doves in the boot of his car that he forgot to release at the church because he was actually in the pub. But it's 'No problemo' for him because, by now, she should be on her honeymoon. Actually she is in hospital, in an exotic location though, with severe dehydration and sun burn. Her mother should persuade him that the bride's nerves are not up to ever hearing about those poor birds – such a bad omen for the marriage. 'What could have been on their poor little minds sitting in that box in the dark in that car for a week?' she should wonder.

The Rules of Making Excuses

Who would willingly attend a wedding? Apart from the bride-to-be, her parents and just maybe the bridesmaids, no one likes to be invited to a wedding. It is probably on a Wednesday because the hotel is offering a midweek polished bronze deal for the happy couple. The only people who don't need an excuse for not turning up are those getting married. Everyone else should have an excuse if they don't intend to show. Ideally, you want an explanation that will allow the couple, if at all possible, to be on speaking terms with you after the wedding. Even though any excuse is unlikely to work, you should make your excuses as an initial tactic to get out of attending. For economy, you can bulk buy your pre-printed gold embossed *Sorry I can't attend your wedding because...* cards. An excuse that has an above-average success rate is one that involves doing voluntary work with the needy. Insert the name of any group of really needy people, not including your mother and clingy mutual friends, in the appropriate space on your card. Alternatively, say you feel you might be developing a terminal illness. You may be dead by the time the happy event comes round. You shouldn't overuse that excuse; ideally you should use it only once and than stay in hiding for the rest of your life. Or you could claim you have to go abroad on urgent business. This should not include holidays but can include accessing highly dangerous life-saving medical procedures and vital organ transplantation; it should not include cosmetic surgery. Say that you are on your way to jail for a five-year term for being caught *in flagrante delicto* in the local cemetery with a fresh corpse. Ideally, every family or group of friends should have a list of who went to what wedding. When you have fulfilled your agreed quota of onerous attendances, you can then nominate someone else to take your place and pretend to be you if necessary. But no matter what your excuse, say you will send a present even though you can't attend yourself.

Excuses that traditionally don't work include claiming that it would cost too much to attend; claiming that you wouldn't enjoy it (why single yourself out – you are not that special); claiming that you don't really enjoy their company and now is as good a time as any to let them know; saying you couldn't be bothered; or claiming you find weddings boring. Remember, you are Irish. Lie to your friends and family because you don't want to upset them with the truth.

The Rules of Giving Presents

If by some miracle you have managed to offer a convincing excuse, you still have to send a present. Cash is good but it shows an unpatriotic unwillingness to avoid any of the traumas of buying a present. Cash is for those who are publicly indicating that they have chosen to drop out of society. The bride-to-be, in consultation with her mother, may decide on a wedding list from Brown Thomas. In this case, you should scramble to get online as fast as you can. Compete for the only four items under a hundred euro, which of course are already gone. Hopefully the bride-to-be may start to feel guilty after one of her relations phones her mother to tell her that she 'can stick her wedding list because she is getting a Sacred Heart picture, same as everyone else.' Following this intervention, the bride-to-be should instruct her mother to inform the guests in general that she is abandoning the idea of a prescribed present list. Ergo, she ends up with five toasters, four deep-fat fryers, two knife blocks, one Sacred Heart picture, three sets of pots, six sets of bed linen, twelve casserole dishes, two Fondue sets, one Le Creuset pot, two woks, four continental quilts, eight coffee pots – one with alarm clock – ten sets of towels, two linen table cloths, five wooden chopping blocks, three sets of knives, one silver canteen, twenty-three figurines, four paintings produced at home by economically inactive guests, one compilation CD, one compromising DVD, eleven thousand eight hundred and fifty-six euro in cash and two hundred and eighty-five euro in dud cheques. From this sum, the bride should spend six hundred and forty-four euro in the bar between 1.30 a.m. and 3.15 a.m. on her wedding night, violently insisting on buying everyone Fluffy Ducks and Boiler Makers.

The Rules of Wedding Pictures

One of the weightier metaphysical dilemmas facing any couple planning their wedding is whether they should record the day, if they must, with still photography or video, or both. This is both sociologically and psychologically interesting because the chosen media reveals a lot about the couple. Control freaks typically choose video because they want everyone to behave in an unnatural way to avoid embarrassment at the subsequent unavoidable wedding-video-viewing party. It is increasingly difficult to avoid seeing yourself in the video because it is usually available to download online. Before accepting an invitation, even to your own wedding, you should seek written guarantees that there will be neither amateur nor professional video evidence available after the event. It is not unreasonable for the couple to instruct the best man, assisted by a team of professional security staff, to frisk all guests at the church for any recording devices including mobile phones. Well-meaning couples will indicate this plan on the wedding invitation.

Still photography is socially more attractive because it demonstrates both taste and empathy on the part of the couple. First, the formal photo shoot allows the plebeian guests to mingle in peace without the bride and groom, family members and other principals, who are obliged to stand outside in the rain, forming a variety of kinship combinations for posterity. Second, still photography allows you to do the same thing over and over again, which, ironically, can make the event go quicker. Professional still photographers have tireless patience. It is not uncommon to hear them say, 'Oh. I missed that. Can you lean over there and smile again? That's better. Thanks. I missed the cutting of the cake. Can you take that piece out of your mouth? Put it back in the cake and cut it again? This time can you try it while smiling? How about stuffing the slice into her mouth? Try her mouth this time instead of her eye. That's great. Now if we can get the mothers in beside the cake. Okay. No problem. We can wait until she comes round. While we are waiting, I have an idea. Just prop her up there. You hold her arm over your shoulder like she is conscious. I have Pritt Stick I can use to keep her eyes open. Very handy. I find that's the great thing about black and white film. You could be dead and no one would notice. Oh. She is dead. Well just lay her in that wonderful shadow over here. I won't use the flash. That's marvelous. Now, if this group could move over there, I could get the next group in. Can you take her with you? Not by the heels – you'll ruin her fascinator. Roll her up in her pashmina. Flower girls in the front here. As I was saying just now, black and white film is wonderful. You won't see the vomit on that dress. Hold still everyone. Say cheese. You. Yes, that small fellow in the velveteen suit with the sweat – what is his name? Jason? Okay, Jason. Don't smile until after you have seen an orthodontist and do it soon. Are we ready? Everyone else smile. Jason, stop crying. Say cheese!'

The Rules for What Counts as a Disaster

It is to be expected that most of the guests will be secretly hoping that something major will go wrong just to break the monotony. Despite the years of planning, things should go wrong. Knowing this, the father of the bride should be seen snorting crushed blood-pressure pills in the side aisle of the church.

Any worthwhile wedding should have at least one disaster. Disasters at weddings are psychologically remarkable phenomena because, no matter what happens, the bride and groom will only be able to remember that they had a great time. In fact, it is always the best wedding they were ever at. One of the most likely places for it all to go wrong is during the after-dinner speeches when the principal orators are under the influence of nerves and alcohol. But disasters can happen before then. Some people think the flower girls crying or the page boys wandering off with the rings is a noteworthy disaster, but any event involving children can only be termed inconvenient rather than catastrophic. Animals are a different matter. There is no excuse for bringing animals to a wedding unless you really cannot leave them behind.

A disaster survivor informed me that her pet cat, Bailey, became completely enmeshed in her elaborate veil and expensive hair-do when he excitedly leaped on to her head as she twirled the ensemble in front of the mirror at home, while preparing for the ceremony. Both Bailey and the bride-to-be became hysterical. They wove each other together in a ball of fur, lace and hair extensions. The bride-to-be's father concluded that the only way to remove Bailey would be to kill him and remove a metre-wide disk of veil and all of the hair on one side of the bride's head. But she loved Bailey too much and, besides, they would have to find a way of killing him that didn't involve bloodshed. She was married while a bridesmaid held the struggling cat in place on her head. After the ceremony, the bride and Bailey went to the vet who performed a successful catectomy, having provided a full anaesthetic for Bailey and tranquilizers for the bride. After Bailey was freed, the bride managed to attend the photo-shoot while the unconscious Bailey was taken home. By standing sideways to the camera and half way behind trees, she managed to almost hide the scratch marks and uneven hair, which you would only notice in the wedding album 'if you were really looking'.

The groom should stand at the altar of the church nervously rehearsing the name of the bride-to-be over and over again, while constantly asking the best man if he still has the rings. When the priest eventually asks for the rings, the best man should search his pockets before remembering that Jason has them balanced on a velvet cushion. Jason, who is a page boy and has been slow-cooking in a dark blue velveteen suit that his mother insisted he wear – because he might catch his death from the drafts in the church – should wake from his dozing and wet his pants in panic. The guests can then start to believe that this day may turn out alright after all.

It is surprising how relatively few brides or grooms fail to turn up for their weddings. But these days it is probably easier to go through a divorce than to work out what to do with the presents. At a wedding I attended recently, the best man made the unprecedented move of standing at the top of the church and asking for our attention. We all went silent in breathless anticipation of a possible major disaster. In our collective imagination, we were already down the pub gossiping about how 'shocked' we were that the bride didn't show, going over in detail the little hints we didn't see at the time – the on-again-off-again relationship; the ring throwing; your one from Donegal that everyone except the bride knew about. 'Ladies and gentlemen, I have an important announcement,' said the best man. We all looked around at each other, struggling to suppress our joy at being firsthand witnesses to a major scandal. 'Can you please turn off your mobile phones during the ceremony?' 'Oh. Is that all?' We reached for our phones in depression as the bride's brother's band started their acoustic version of Wagner's 'Bridal Chorus' from *Lohengrin* to signal that the bride had actually shown up.

At a wedding in the midlands, a large bride had herself sewn into her under-sized dress along the side seam under her arm. Both her and the extraordinary long train were carefully folded into the antique Rolls-Royce that was to take her to the church. Somewhere on the way, she had a violent argument with her father. When the car pulled up, she opened the door and ran straight into the church in a sulk. Her distracted and embarrassed father, rushing to catch up and be at least beside her as she galloped up the aisle, slammed the door on the end of her train. She was just inside the doors of the church and making good speed when the dress split and came off in one piece, leaving her standing there in her new lingerie with matching suspender belt and knickers. The guests were delighted that they had shown up for *that* wedding. Following the delay involved in sewing her back into the dress, the wedding proceeded as planned. And some brides complain that you can see the bridesmaid's bra strap in the video when she is dancing with the best man.

The Rules of Speech Making

One of the most enjoyable weddings I was at was the one where the father of the bride selflessly had a heart attack during the soup course. The rest of the dinner was cancelled, along with the speeches. We were profoundly grateful.

Tailor-made wedding speeches and tutorials are available to download from the internet for each of the participants who are obliged to address the unhappy guests as their digestive juices battle with the Wicklow venison or cauliflower curry. Speeches usually range from premium to platinum. You get what you pay for. I prefer to listen to platinum speeches in which you can clearly see where the extra investment has gone. Each of these speech tutorials come with a guide to what the speaker should and shouldn't do. In terms of advisable length of speech, some websites suggest that you can allow seasoned speechifiers up to forty minutes' speaking time. It is easy to imagine every speaker, drunk on the initial applause and alcohol, convincing themselves that they are the very best public speakers the unhappy guests may ever hear in their lives. With these tutorials, expect the speakers to drone on for hours.

The Do's of Public Speaking

I will give you an anthropological summary of the professional advice available online, which I have localised to a specifically Irish wedding speech context. This advice falls under the headings of what you should do and what you should not do. You are advised to make a list of each with clear headings. That is fine advice when sober but confusing when not. Because weddings are definitely sentimental

81

occasions, we are advised, if called upon to make a speech, to emphasise how important and special the bride and groom are to us. If you are the groom, you should be prepared to say how important the bride is to you, and vice versa. At an Irish wedding you should not take it for granted that your audience will have made this connection. If you are the father of the bride, you should tell your audience how happy you are to welcome a new member into your family. You should not say how particularly happy you are that it is actually the person sitting in front of you and not the rich, professionally qualified responsible one with whom you got on so well, but who dumped your daughter six months ago after he found her in bed with someone who is also not the peron sitting in front of you today. Apparently, professional speechwriters do not encourage jokes on that theme, even if they are true. On the other hand, neither are you encouraged to over-state your affection for your new son-in-law in your speech, because, by doing so, you may raise suspicions of insincerity on your part. Wedding guests are a tough crowd, especially while digesting Wicklow venison.

We are also advised that looking confident is being confident. Therefore, while speaking, you should both smile and make eye contact with your audience. This means that you don't stare at the bride's cleavage because you know the difference between smiling and drunken leering. For the Irish speaker, this distinction poses subtle epistemological challenges. For the Irish wedding, to be on the safe side, I recommend that all the speechmakers practise together in front of the mirror in the gents' toilet before going live. Practise smiling, making charismatic eye contact and avoiding leering.

The professional speechwriters also advise that you slow down. But this advice presents specific contextual challenges. To produce a good slow and steady pace in an Irish speaker, it is well accepted that he or she should consume a measured amount of alcohol to avoid our natural logor-rhoea. However, everyone knows that alcohol gives rise to leering and staring, so you will need to get the precise balance just right. Experienced best men – with a reputation for the most memorable speeches – being of average build and weight, recommend three glasses of Champagne, four pints of lager, two and a half glasses of red wine, four glasses of white wine, two rum and blacks, and a double malted whisky, followed by a ten-minute rehearsal in front of the toilet mirror, before taking the microphone. You can add one unit of alcohol for each inch above six feet you stand in your socks. If in doubt, you can remove your shoes in the gents and ask someone to measure you while you lie along a convenient wall.

It is also recommended that you stand still while speak-ing, which in my experience as a wedding guest is very sound advice that is often ignored. Standing still makes it easier for a group of guests to grab the speaker if required. You should also breathe in and out (without actually saying 'breathe in and out'). After alcohol, forgetting to breathe is the single most important contributing factor to the speaker blacking out.

It is recommended that you bring in an anecdote relat-ing to your earliest memory of the bride or groom when they were young, which gave you an insight into what they would be like when grown up. For example, if you are a parent you can refer nostalgically to some exchange you had with your son or daughter; or, if you and your bride/groom are childhood sweethearts, you can recall your first meeting as children. But remember, you are Irish. Do this in the spirit of having moved on. You have put that day behind you. After twelve years of counselling, you are over it.

You are also advised to mean what you say because, alleg-edly, the room is charged with good will, love and happiness. Because this advice is idealised, you need to adjust it to your specific guest list. The best man should take this opportunity to tell the bride how much he 'really loves her, yes really, like, really loves her. Not, like, loves her but really loves her. Always has, since the first day the groom brought her back to the flat they shared...' If this isn't working, the best man might decide to ignore the breathe-in-and-out advice and go for a tactical blackout. With all that honesty in the air, it is also an ideal opportunity for the father of the bride to announce his intention to leave the mother of the bride because he really, really loves Bernie from down the road. It is also a good time to shed a few tears. As a member of the audience at many of these events, I find crying very therapeutic.

Finally, you are advised that you should be yourself!

If you are in the crowd, do sneak out to the bar and return three hours later when the speeches have ended. Speeches traditionally end a half hour after the last collective gasp of dismay is heard in the bar from the dining room.

The Don'ts of Public Speaking

When speaking in public, frequently remove your list of what you shouldn't do from your pocket. Study it carefully, committing its contents to memory. The first item on your list should be a reminder to actually *not* be yourself. It is not the occasion on which to announce your existential insights into the nature of your true political ideology, sexuality or your own existence in general. In traditional Irish fashion, try to be someone else for ten minutes.

The problem with having a list of things that you shouldn't do or say is that, under the stresses of the occasion, you may become confused between those things you should do and those that you promised yourself you wouldn't do. The problem with don'ts is that, once you have been handed a long list of them by the groom, the mother-of-the-bride, the bride and bridesmaids, confusion can set in, especially if there was any miscalculations in your intake of alcohol, prescribed for slowing down your natural manic speaking velocity.

Further down the list it should say: 'Don't be crude or smutty.' This generally means not detailing any sexual partners of either the bride or groom in the past or present. In particular, you should not relate the story about how 'When we all went away together on a camping holiday, I was going at it with the bridesmaid in a sleeping bag in my tent – well, I thought it was her because it was pitch black – and then, when she came into the tent with a flashlight, I said, 'I wonder who this is', and I looked down and – ha ha – wasn't it only the bride herself. Jaysus, how we laughed.'

Don't forget to substitute the names in the internet speech with the names of the other main characters at your wedding. Remember, you are not marrying Julie and your father is not Seamus, as far as you know.

* * *

When I got married, my sister threw the rice so hard at us as we came out of the church that I had to seek medical assistance to have a grain removed from my eye. Whoever heard of rice at an Irish wedding? My brother-in-law, who drove our wedding car, was bursting to go to the toilet so he drove away from the church so fast that most of our guests got lost. Many never made it to the reception but ended up in a nearby pub where, apparently, the craic was great. This wouldn't have happened if we had had a professionally driven Rolls-Royce instead of a diesel saloon that had been a temporary home to a pair of calves.

Next day, when we drove off on our honeymoon, we were obliged to pick up three of our guests who were thumbing their way home in the snow. Best wedding ever. Everyone had a great time!

5

Health: Overheard in the Waiting Room

[The Irish] is one race of people for whom psycho-analysis is of no use whatsoever.

(Sigmund Freud)

Medical anthropologists study health and disease patterns, and there is no hard evidence that they all failed to get into medical school. Medical anthropologists see beyond biology and recognise that people become ill within a cultural environment. Patients differ because they belong to different cultures and experience their illnesses differently. In an Irish context, we get fat, we don't take exercise, and we smoke and drink too much. And we do our best to deny we have anything wrong with us until the very last possible moment, which is usually in the ambulance.

You can't be Irish just by wishing the condition on yourself. You have to work on adopting our national characteristics, one of which is the way in which we deal with illness. If you really want to be Irish, there are a range of traditional Irish diseases available to you. Some of the very Celtic ones you will need to have been born with, like haemochromatosis, but the others you will be able to develop for yourself. These range from depression, or should I say misery, to heart disease and diabetes. My own personal favourite is hypochondria, because that allows you to have them all, sometimes simultaneously. Mammies can play a central role in Irish mental health and diet, so you may have to get yourself an Irish mammy right away. Try an adoption agency. As we will see, there are lots of child-less couples that would gladly take you on.

I am interested in the topic of medicine because I am a hypochondriac. When their doctor tells an Irish hypochon-driac that they are dying, they are unlikely to query the accuracy of the result, being more comfortable with our national fatalism. If told they are fine, they will usually question the accuracy of the diagnosis. Even if they become convinced that they are okay, they know anything could happen on the way home from the clinic. If my long-suffer-ing GP tells me I am fine, I am likely to conclude that he just couldn't be bothered helping me with the funeral arrange-ments. Not his job really.

The other face of hypochondria is denial. If you are not actually imagining every possible affliction, you should be actively ignoring that head-sized lump growing on your neck. If you want to be Irish, you have to know how to be sick like an Irish person. You have to learn how to balance the baseless fatalism of hypochondria against the ground-less optimism of denial.

In order to find out how Irish people suffer, both mentally and physically, I decided to hang out with members of the medical profession, the ones who actually got into medical school.

* * *

In general, Irish people talk continuously about a seemingly endless array of topics. However, there are definite taboo subjects, even in a hospital. If you are an exhibitionist, you might mention that you are constipated, for example, but only as a hint to the paramedics before passing out. Likewise, while you are allowed to tell haemorrhoid-based jokes, you would never make reference to your own piles. However, within the privacy of your own family, you can discuss your genes. Our particular way of complaining about each other would not be possible without our strong commitment to the role of genetics in influencing our everyday behaviour. This is an example of the superior influence of nature over the nurturing effects of parenting. Responsible Irish parents are usually able to trace the influence of at least four generations of genes on their children's behaviour. Genetics covers everything from your life expectancy to your personality and your good or bad luck. For example, in my own case, my mother's family had a reputation for coronary disease, or dodgy tickers, while my father's family, though long living, tended to be mad. When I was about ten, my mother sat me down to tell me that I was old enough to know the truth. She informed me that two possible genetic roads lay ahead for me. On the one hand, I could live to be a hundred, but most of those years would be ruined by insanity. On the other hand, she said, tapping her sternum, if I was lucky, I might die young from a massive heart attack with my wits still intact.

For Irish children growing up in this highly scientific environment, it is common to hear a parent say, 'You get that from your [insert the name of a member of the other parent's family].' If you've strangled the cat, your mother will say: 'Your father's side of the family were all peculiar around animals. There was your Uncle Tom, your father's brother, who had to be sent away when he was twelve for what he did to that poor sheep. That sheep was never the same after. No one could bring themselves to eat one bite of it.' When Irish children do something praiseworthy, they are reminded by a parent of the outstanding achievements of that parent's family. Typically, that parent will say, 'I am not surprised that you solved Fermat's Last Theorem. Wasn't your uncle, my brother, great at mental arithmetic.'

Children in single-parent families miss out on much of this because they lack competing genetic role models. Also, children who are lucky enough to be raised in orphanages remain ignorant of their genetic inheritance.

The Rules of Confession

Sigmund Freud had this much in common with Catholicism: he believed that sex was the cause of all emotional problems. Traditionally in Ireland, when we wanted to talk to a complete stranger about sex, we went to confession. Confession was very good value because it allowed you forgiveness, not just for past transgressions, but for future ones as well. You just asked the priest to forgive 'these and all my other sins [the ones you haven't mentioned]' – and it was free. However, afterwards very few of us were willing to talk about what we said in confession.

Your psychotherapist's clinic has replaced the confession box as the place to talk about yourself to people who have to listen. While going to confession was never hip, and few boasted about the sins they confessed, psychotherapy, which is now very popular in Ireland, is cool.

You can increase your social cachet with appropriate hints about your emotional imbalance. A sophisticated range of neuroses has replaced good old-fashioned guilt caused by having too much sex, having not enough sex, thinking about sex too much or not thinking about it often enough. In contemporary Ireland, it is acceptable to be neurotic as a form of social style. Your particular form of neurosis is very much dependent on your social aspirations. There is a counselling or psychotherapeutic approach for all your ambitions. If you have no friends, or your nearest and dearest have lost all patience with your obsessive single-minded moaning, you can take yourself along to an analyst. When you go for analysis, you should be prepared to talk dirty because we know from Freud that all madness is about sex. Of course, you have to pay. Prostitutes are reluctant to waste their time chitchatting with a client. When you go to the analyst, you can spend the whole time just talking about sex.

Many Irish people feel that this is an essential service because they have limited opportunities for talking about sex in ordinary conversation. If you are socialising in polite Irish society, it is considered gauche to talk openly about sex. However, at an appropriate pause in conversation, between trays of canapés and Hendrix gin with a slice of cucumber, you can subliminally talk about sex by re-starting the conversation with the sentence: 'I don't know how I will cope because my analyst is out of the country for the next month.' Don't say, 'My analyst advised me to get in touch with my inner me,' because everyone knows analysts don't advise. They just listen. Counsellors advise, but only people with embarrassing and practical problems see counsellors. Be prepared for someone to ask, 'Is your analyst a Lacanian or a Kleinian?', a question which demonstrates their sophisticated and nuanced insight. In answer, mutter something about the need for confidentiality and your worry that you may have already said too much.

I consulted a psychiatrist for my research. He told me that the Irish mammy was almost single-handedly responsible for most Irish male mental disorders. (Poor Irish mammies are blamed for everything!) Officially, your Irish mother will drive you crazy. My psychiatrist told me of a 55-year-old man who had lived with his mammy all his life. In a reversal of roles, he took his mother to the doctor after she started exhibiting symptoms of dementia. He was frustrated because his domestic harmony was being disturbed by her behaviour. The doctor told him that his mother had Alzheimer's. The son told the doctor that it was very difficult for him to come to terms with the fact that, after fifty-five years of her looking after him, it was now his turn to look after his mother. The doctor asked if he had any questions. He had just one – could the doctor recommend a good nursing home where he could send her?

Misery Is Not just for Christmas

Misery is very common in Ireland. If you want to feel part of the crowd, you should work on your own depression. Depression is fairly easily acquired. The best way to become chronically depressed is to follow a few well-tested procedures. In no time at all, you will be one of us. The following is a brief self-hindrance programme I put together with the help of my psychiatrist. It helps if you can get a close family member or a friend involved from the beginning to undermine your confidence and determination as you go along.

In order to experience authentic Irish depressive episodes, the last thing you will want to do when you start to feel really down is to talk to anyone, especially anyone who can help. If you do that, you will ruin the low you can achieve. Remember that being Irish means that you don't confide your problems to anyone because your problems are unique. Keep in mind that, in the history of human kind, no one has ever felt the way you do now. After all, your mammy has told you how special you are. Remember, this is Ireland: there is no help out there. Money problems, marital problems, anxiety about leaving the house, obsessions about electrical switches and if you really turned off the cooker, worrying about your son ending up in jail, that mysterious lump on your neck – any one of these things could be unique to you. To discuss it with anyone else would be ridiculous, an assault on our long-held traditions.

You will have no chance of reaching the depths of despair if you go to the doctor. Remember, she can't help you because she is only useful if you are actually sick. For fast and effective results, do the following:

- Hang out with people who are only interested in themselves.
- Never deal with a problem today that you can think about tomorrow.
- Drink loads of alcohol, because a) alcohol makes all real problems go away and b) alcohol helps the depression get worse.
- If you are eventually carried bodily to the doctor, lie as much as you can and don't take the pills. They will only make you feel better. Remember, we're Irish. We don't like feeling good because it makes us feel guilty. But that's good because guilt leads to depression.

The Rules of Losing Weight

It is also popular to become miserable over your weight. Weight gain in Ireland is often the result of health fads such as taking exercise and quitting smoking. Exercise causes injuries and injuries lead to sitting around the house consolation eating. My psychiatrist told me that many of us comfort eat because the Great Potato Famine of the 1840s is buried deep in our psyches. Many of us even look like potatoes. Quitting smoking causes weight gain that in turn leads to yo-yo dieting. As an Irish person, you have a choice between dying skinny or fat. You choose.

We avoid fish probably because it is good for us. If you see a fish coming, run. If you go to dinner in someone else's house, it is customary to say, just before your plate is placed on the table in front of you, 'Oh, did I tell you I don't eat fish. Never eat them actually. Hate them. I don't agree with the cruelty involved in catching them. Think of the poor dolphins getting caught up in the tuna nets. Dolphins are just so intelligent and giving. They are smarter than people really.' If you are serving the tuna, resist saying, 'Speak for yourself.' If you are Irish, do say, 'That's no problem. I'll just put on a few fish fingers for you.'

If you are rich, serious about losing weight and you really want results, you can try liposuction. It works every time, if you regain consciousness. Or you can hire someone to manage your weight for you, and engage in one-on-one motivational sessions.

If an Irish person is serious about losing weight and keeping it off, they can join Weight Watchers for life and subject themselves to the spur of public humiliation.

At Weight Watchers, you have just six weeks before you have to get into that white jump suit or that white wedding dress. Remember, in the words of one team leader, 'A dream is just a dream, but a goal is a dream with a plan and a deadline. Remember that "desserts" is "stressed" spelt backwards.' Weight Watchers routinely changes its points system to keep you on your toes; if you get confused, you can buy yourself a points calculator. Or you can use an app to keep track. The point is to become utterly obsessed. Here are a few Weight Watchers recipes that I picked up:

Take a tin of tomato soup, which has practically zero points; add two spoons of curry powder. Serve with rice and, hey presto, you have a curry. Or take a can of Weight Watchers mushroom soup and serve over pasta topped with low-low cheddar cheese – gorgeous and practically food. You can eat as many tomatoes as you like. If you don't like tomatoes, you can eat anything else you like as long as you jog while eating it. It is an important tradition to break out while dieting. Just one packet of biscuits will provide all the points you need to go over your daily allowance without eating anything else. Once you have scoffed the biscuits, you may as well go mad and just start all over again tomorrow.

You can also purge yourself with emetics. According to a doctor I consulted, the singer Enya is quite an effective emetic and is responsible for acute episodes of nausea, vomiting and diarrhoea, often attributed to some blameless bacterium. If you want to lose weight, put on those CDs now.

Grow Your Own Beer Belly

Loads of Irish people have beer bellies, even men, so don't be left out. In fact, the beer belly is one of our most ubiquitous national symbols. Growing your own is very fashionable. A beer belly can be achieved by drinking beer. However, chips, curries, bacon rolls, Taytos, Cadbury's chocolate, ice-cream and big feeds of hairy bacon will also help. A beer belly is handy because you can, for example, rest a can of beer on it, leaving your hands free for scoffing fish and chips or to operate the remote control for the telly.

The ideal beer belly should stick straight out at a right angle to your body. If your beer belly hangs pendulously over your belt, you can make it firmer by stuffing in more beer and curries. Your beer belly should prevent you from seeing anything below your navel, which is essentially a valve to prevent you from actually bursting. Sex becomes impossible for the beer belly couple, allowing them more time for eating and drinking.

Having a beer belly is an essential Celtic prelude to the next stage of Irish integration – having an Irish heart attack. Happily, according to medical science, having the one often leads to the other.

A Twelve-Step Guide to Having an Irish Heart Attack

An informant, who will remain nameless, told me about his heart attack, which was so typical of the Irish male experience that we formulated a guide together in case you, too, would like to be typically Irish in this regard.

Our twelve-step guide to the Irish heart attack is designed for Irish men. While women may follow the steps, I am not guaranteeing results. The guide ignores the important role of the Irish breakfast and breakfast roll. For best results, you should have at least one full Irish breakfast with extra black pudding every morning for about five years, with everything fried in Cookeen, followed by a breakfast roll with four sausages for elevenses. Avoid all exercise.

So, here is an easy-to-follow guide to having an Irish heart attack:

Step One: Ignore the pain in your chest for at least three weeks; ideally for as long as you can.

Step Two: After a large evening meal, preferably involving at least four courses, including a grand feed of cabbage and hairy bacon with parsley sauce, lovely floury potatoes and a bottle of wine, head to the pub and consume eight pints of lager, a half bottle of wine, four packets of crisps and two packets of dry roasted peanuts. Stop for a curry and chips on the way home. Shake all the above together into a smooth constituency in your beer belly at a house party next door. Add extra liquid as required and retire to bed.

Step Three: Wake in the middle of the night with a violent pain in your chest.

Step Four: Grope your way along the floor into the bathroom. Take four Rennie or drink a quarter bottle of Maalox, whichever you have to hand. Wait ten minutes and repeat the dose.

Step Five: Return to bed. Lie absolutely still, waiting for the pain to go away. While waiting, pray to your favourite saint for a miracle. Vow to mend your ways in the morning if your prayers are answered.

Step Six: Repeat steps four and five.

Step Seven: Sit on the end of the bed for exactly one hour, groaning and sweating. If you are of a mind, review your life's achievements. This task will be facilitated by your life flashing before your glassy eyes.

Step Eight: When your wife is eventually awakened by the noise, she should sleepily ask if you are all right. Say that you are fine; that you are just having a think.

Step Nine: Repeat steps four through seven for as many times as required until your wife wakes up again. This time she should tell you she is definitely calling an ambulance. You should continue to protest how fine you are and ask her not to be making a fuss about nothing. Because your wife says she has decided to call the ambulance, you concede that you will walk to the hospital.

Step Ten: Walk to the car, lie across the back seat and allow yourself to be driven to A&E.

Step Eleven: Walk into A&E complaining about 'all this fuss for nothing'. Wonder aloud how you are going to live down the mortification when they find nothing wrong with you. Claim that you may die from that embarrassment.

Step Twelve: Pass out.

The only sure-fire way to be certain that you are having a massive fatal coronary episode is to wait to read about it in the obituary notices in the *Indo*, where you will be listed under the 'suddenlys'.

The Rules of Ageing

For the older Irish man or woman who foregoes the more traditional choice of fatal heart attack or massive stroke, there is still the option of type 2 diabetes, which is currently the rage. Back when we were all too poor to live to be old, only the elite could achieve diabetes. Now it is within practically every Irish person's reach.

Test Rules

It is important not to have any tests when you do eventually go to the doctor, because he may find something wrong. If you don't get something tested, you will never be sure whether you have something or not. Therefore, it is best not to get the test. If, God forbid, you get a positive result, well, you are finished. You know then that you are going to die. You are better off praying and waiting to see what happens. If you are going to die, it is important to die of the right thing. No one in Ireland wants to die from cancer. Anything else will do.

Overheard in the Waiting Room

To find out how being ill works in practice, I needed to meet sick people, or at least people who thought they were sick. Perhaps because he didn't know what anthropologists did, Dr A agreed to allow me to hang out in his very busy practice. I was to spend the mornings in reception, followed by sitting in the waiting room in the afternoons chatting with the patients. I was hardly sitting down behind reception when my first patient turned up. He was an hour early for his appointment.

'You are an hour early,' I tell him, worried that I am misinterpreting some vital information in my new job.

'That's right. I like waiting.'

'Okay then. Wait in the waiting room.'

My next patient comes in. 'I have an appointment.'

'Do you?'

'Do I? At what time?'

'I'll take over this one,' C, the real receptionist, helpfully tells me, shoving me out of the way.

Later in the morning, C hands a patient a prescription. She tells her that the dose of her medication has been increased. The patient seems pleased. C explains to me that the dose has actually been decreased, but she knew that that particular patient wouldn't be happy to hear that she is getting better.

Working on reception, I realise that I don't know what I am doing. I confess my ignorance and am sent to restock the shelves that hold the vital forms that keep the practice running smoothly. In the storeroom, I am piling armfuls of large envelopes, small envelopes and disability certificates into a box. When I come upon a pile of blank death certificates, I feel a shudder down my spine and hurry back to reception where the banter with the patients continues.

'I am worried about taking a stroke,' a new arrival at reception informs me.

When a patient tells me that she is looking for a cert for breaking her arm, I stupidly ask when she is going to break it. She shows me the cast while shaking her head at me.

Everyone seems to be having blood tests. I warn them to fast before coming in in the morning for their blood to be taken.

A patient tells me to tell the doctor she is in the toilet if she is called, because she has to go outside for a fag: 'Listen – if she calls "Nichola", tell her I'm in the loo, will ya? Tanks.'

The phone rings. The voice on the other end tells me it's an emergency. 'I can't get my breath. I can't walk down the road to get my fags.' When the patient turns up at reception an hour later, she has her daughter with her as part of a general domestic-wide emergency.

'What is your name?' I ask another patient.

'Bridie!'

'Bridie who?'

'Bridie Bridie.'

'Take a seat,' I tell her. This is another one for the real receptionist.

After lunch, I sit in the waiting room combining eaves-dropping with small talk for a different kind of ethnographic experience. It is a strange feeling to expect to spend all after-noon in a room designed for a tense twenty-minute wait. It is not easy to confront a waiting patient about their illness or inquire what brings them to see the doctor. After a while, I discover that patients fall into two camps. One type of patient is extremely reticent, and sits silently, staring straight ahead, rehearsing their worries to themselves over and over with do-not-disturb expressions on their faces. The other type is extremely forthcoming, very happy to publicise their entire medical history at the slightest sign of my interest. They enjoy their ill health. They relish a new audient who hasn't heard it all before. Fortunately for my research, the latter type of patient forms the majority in the waiting room.

The skill is to decide which type I may be dealing with when they come in. Sometimes the more reticent ones will talk. I experiment with a few probing questions. If 'Do you come here often?' gets a smile, I'm in. If not, I'm out. Over the following days, I perfect my technique.

A woman comes in with a white plaster on her nose. 'What are you here for?' I ask, figuring that this could be one of the lighter conversations. 'My blood pressure,' she answers. After a full minute of silent staring at me, she continues, 'and I have a tumour on my nose.'

A conversation breaks out elsewhere. 'It's a disgrace. I have been here twenty minutes. Did you see Liz Taylor?

Left a billion. All those rich husbands. That was a sting job. All those marriages. Like this place. A sting job. Once your health goes, they clean you out before they let you die. Drain you dry. Blood money. You pay to let them take the blood out of you. It's a disgrace.'

The room fills with a general chatter. Suddenly, for no obvious reason, everyone falls silent at the same moment and stares at the floor. After a few minutes, a mobile phone ringing and a bout of lung-churning coughing breaks the silence.

By now, because I am a hypochondriac, I have developed a serious concern about catching something in the waiting room. I use the steriliser dispenser a lot. I try to control my hypochondria. I realise that rushing into the doctor myself for help would be a methodological embarrassment for all anthropologists.

An elderly man sits down beside me. I ask him what brings him to the doctor.

'I am only here for my MOT. There is nothing the matter with me. I am not on any pills. I am here to get my ears syringed.' After two minutes of silence, he continues unprompted: 'I'm just on one little white pill. The first time, they gave me one big one. That was after my suicide attempt. Now I am on just the one small white one. Then I am on two for the blood pressure. One to counteract the other. One pill makes the pressure go up. The other makes it come down again. One was making me woozy, but when I forgot to take the other one I was fine. I managed to fix myself. Then there is the pill for the borderline diabetes. How many is that?'

I consult my notes. 'That's four, if you count both blood pressure pills.'

'Then I had to have the brain scan. The missus is on a bag with bowel cancer. But she is fine. She managed to hold on to her hair.'

'I am glad there is nothing wrong with you,' I tell him before sliding along the bench to eavesdrop on two young women who have come in together. I hear one telling the other that her chest is killing her: 'If we have to wait, I am going to have to have a ciggie.'

There is a woman in the corner compulsively cleaning her baby's toy. Her neighbour, a mother with a seven-year-old boy, confidently advises her on the likelihood that her baby will be admitted to hospital. 'If I was you, I would go straight to the Children's Hospital in Temple Street.' Her own son is sitting on the floor. 'Get up and go into the toilet and wash your hands,' she tells him. 'The place is full of germs.'

'But I am just here for the vaccination,' the other mother tells her.

'Doesn't matter. Head straight to the hospital. You will end up there anyway.' Her son returns to tell her that he couldn't reach the tap. He picks up a toy and sticks it in his mouth. Immediately, he is back in the toilet with a wooden toy box to stand on so he can reach the sink.

'I am going to tell the doctor that he isn't right,' his mother says. 'He did his first confession last week and the teacher didn't even turn up. Get blood tests. Lots of blood tests.' We all lapse into silence while we contemplate the meaning of her comments. The child is back playing with the toys, which are now strewn all over the floor. I sanitise my hands just in case.

In reception, a patient comes in to see any doctor. When I ask him what is the matter, he tells me that there is nothing the matter with him. He has a medical card and he wants to make as much use of it as possible. I tell him he will have to wait because he hasn't an appointment.

A woman comes in with a child. She tells me that she was here yesterday with her other child, but today this child needs to see the doctor. It seems that, if you can't be sick yourself, you can have a family member be sick for you. When she tells me that she has three children, I am confident I will see her again tomorrow.

The phone rings. A man wants to see a lady doctor.
'Which one?' I ask.
'The one I saw before.'
'Which one is that?'
'I don't remember her name.'
'What did she look like?'
'I don't remember.'
'Was she blonde?'
'I don't know. All I remember is that she was very nice.'
'I'll put you in for a very nice doctor at eleven twenty tomorrow.'
'Thanks.' I feel I am making progress.

Another patient comes in. 'I am here for my sick cert,' she tells me. 'I'm on the sick.'
'What is wrong with you?'
'Me back. Haven't worked in years.'
I ask her for her PPS number, which she knows off by heart. I flirt with the idea of stealing a pad of sickie notes for my own use.

'I need a prescription. NOW!' someone else shouts at me.

I notice that the lower down the social ladder the patients are, the less stoical they are about small complaints, while they bear the big problems with great courage. A patient with a backache makes his way up the stairs incredibly slowly for his appointment. I ask if I can help, but he rejects my offer. He carefully places both feet onto each step before progressing to the next. A few minutes later, he comes bounding down the stairs with a prescription. I am very impressed with the powers of the doctor upstairs.

A letter comes in on a bookmaker's docket. Clearly our patient found time between bets to reflect on his state of health as well as the state of his wealth. The letter explains that the author could not get out of the house because he had put his back out. He needed a resupply of Solpadeine. A used box is attached for reference.

In the waiting room, two women with crutches come in together. One brushes her hair compulsively while they talk. I learn that they are friends who met through their disability. They share the firm conviction that men are horrible. They hobble off together into the consulting room when called.

A woman tells me that she got a new hip for Christmas in Tallaght Hospital. 'They made a balls of it. Got an infection. Was in agony. My hip was completely black. Jaysus, the pain was unbelievable. I am back in hospital tomorrow to have it whipped out and a new one put in. I'm going to make sure they don't give me one of those dodgy French ones.' A name is called and she limps off. She is replaced by a suspected kidney stone.

A young, pale couple arrive. She is here for a pregnancy test. He looks extremely worried. Perhaps he is wondering if he is really the father. Should he run away now? She sits near the door to block any escape. They are the unhappiest looking couple I have ever seen.

Later in the afternoon, a mother is waiting with her son Jason, aged six. Jason is sitting on the floor trying to do his homework. He shows his efforts to his mother who tells him that he is great. She gives him a sweet. Jason looks around at us, smugly chewing his reward. She proudly tells everyone waiting that Jason has diabetes, asthma, eczema, is lactose intolerant and coeliac, and cannot play sports in school.

The waiting room is a day out for some families, with mother, father and all the siblings coming along. A family consisting of a grandmother, her son and daughter-in-law, granddaughter and two grandsons take up one wall and wait in total silence together. When they all go in to see the doctor as a group, I am left to wonder if they have some form of contagious disease. Could this be a case of extended family Munchausen syndrome? After a quick hand wash with the sanitiser, I am fine again.

I change subject matter. I question the older waiting patients about their views on the best way to stay healthy. A woman tells me that lifestyle and prayer keep her going. 'You don't have to go to Lourdes to pray. You can pray anywhere. I only drink at the weekends and I don't believe in exercise.'

An elderly man tells me that he hasn't been to the doctor in forty-six years: 'I just got a bit panicky during the cold spell. I put my good health down to hard work and plain living.'

Elderly couples come in together. They usually sit side by side in total silence, because they have nothing left to say to each other. Perhaps the women are thinking fondly of a time when they thought that their husbands would be dead by this age. They agreed to stay together until death did they part, but he is taking it at bit far at this stage. Look at Mrs Murphy. Out every night at bingo enjoying herself since her fella died.

The Rules of Having an Irish Baby

Socially, it is likely to happen, usually during dinner, that some couple will tell you they are 'trying for a baby', or that they 'would do anything for a baby'. Do not become alarmed because, surprisingly, sex doesn't form part of their efforts: they are not about to take up a position amongst the plates on the table. They will tell you that they have tried everything, including sex standing on their heads, but have now moved on to science. You will also notice that they have abandoned the general reticence we ordinary Irish have about everything below the waist, and will provide you with a fully illustrated gynaecological history. Never invite a couple trying for a baby to dinner. In fact, don't let them into your house. In the interest of research, I sought out a couple trying desperately for a baby to see how it worked.

It all starts on the honeymoon. The couple look at each other in panic. They unconsciously decide to have children in order to hide from each other. Children will distract them for the fifty-three years it will take them to leave home. Desperate sex follows and nothing happens. But it is easier to keep trying than to get a divorce when they get home.

Women control the business end of having babies. If a couple are having difficulty conceiving, the first step is to eliminate the possibility that it might be the man's fault. The woman should have sex with someone at work who agrees to a sex-only relationship on the desk every evening after work for six weeks. The woman should pick someone from the willing candidates who has the same hair colour and a passing resemblance to her husband. If, after six weeks, she fails to become pregnant, she should inform her husband that she is having herself checked out.

I spoke with a woman who had been trying for a baby for ten years. Her obsession started by accident when she had an unplanned ectopic pregnancy that ended in her recovering in a maternity hospital. After having a fallopian tube removed, she was wandering around the hospital in a depression when she came across a pregnant seventeen-year-old in a pink nylon dressing gown, smoking a fag outside the front door. She said to my informant: 'We all heard about you, luv. You're the one with the baby trapped in the tube. You poor thing.' Putting out the cigarette with her foot, she continued: 'I have to go drop this one. It's kicking the shit out of me. See ya!' Enraged by the biological injustice of the world, there and then my informant resolved that, no matter what it took, she was going to have a baby. After a lot of prodding and poking by the doctors, she started on a course of IVF.

IVF consists of two things: years of tracking cycles, hormonal nasal sprays, injections and egg implants, and advice that you get from your well-meaning friends and family. The opinions of others are almost as painful as the medical procedures. The most common advice is for the couple to just relax. My informant was not impressed: 'How can you relax when your mother-in-law tells you about the couple who just relaxed and had five sprogs in a row?' Acupuncture, Chinese herbs, damp heat, enemas and pine-apples[11] also supposedly work wonders. When not giving advice, mothers-in-law ask if there is 'any news'? The standard reply is to shout 'No. No fucking news', to which the standard response is 'You have to learn to relax. Julie-down-the-road's cousin's girlfriend was trying for five years and then she just relaxed. Maybe ye are allergic to each other.'

During IVF treatments, men have fun and women suffer. My informant told me that she became addicted to IVF after twelve cycles, each lasting eight weeks, where you get to inject yourself like a junkie, snort hormones to stimulate your ovaries, and take your eggs out, fertilise them, put them back in and wait two weeks. This is the famous TWW.[12] You find out it didn't work but that means you can start all over again. You meet fellow addicts in the IVF waiting rooms. You exchange stories of near misses, egg counts and how you were nearly busted for having a carload of syringes. You have taken up crime to support your egg habit. You break into houses to pay for the treatments. You hold up all-night petrol stations. Your fella drives the getaway car because it is better than listening to your insane mutterings about natural births at home when he is trying to watch the football on the telly.

---

[11] I don't know what you are supposed to do with the pineapple.
[12] TWW stands for the *Two Weeks' Wait*. It takes two weeks to confirm whether or not the egg implant has worked.

After the stress of ten years trying for a baby, the couple are usually so exhausted and so poor that they couldn't be bothered separating. They agree that the easiest thing to do is to adopt a baby.

The Rules of Adoption

No ordinary Irish family would qualify for adoption. To qualify, you have to be extraordinary because you don't want some poor orphan ending up with a typical Irish family. To be eligible to adopt, you have to wait on a list for three years. Then your application is activated after you are subjected to garda clearance. Next, you have to do a course in parenting and you have to get married to your partner. You can adopt in a cohabiting relationship, but if a couple splits up the child goes with the person whose name is on the adoption papers; it's like a joint account – best to have two signatories in case of a fight. Then the social worker calls to your house to check that you are normal. You should think long and hard about your answers to their questions. Remember, you have to appear normal by the standards of Irish social workers. Have your wedding photo album on display on the sideboard. Be prepared to address such questions as 'Did you get married for love or to have a baby?', 'How is your sex life?', 'Is there a history of alcoholism or depression in your family?' The answer to all such questions is 'No. We are actually from Belgium.'

When you get through this, you get a declaration of eligibility. You can now get a catalogue to see what kind of baby you might like. Since there are practically no Irish babies available, someone will suggest for you to go abroad. You are advised to choose a country about which you have no negative preconceptions whatsoever. For example, you are advised that if you don't like the food of a particular country, don't adopt a child from there. My informant's efforts were set back two years when she suggested to her social worker that she would like a brown one to match her sofa.

Pity the poor orphan who has to live up to the expectations of fourteen years of manic effort to acquire him or her.

* * *

Dr A brings me to his Monday morning clinic at the Homeless Hostel. It is cold and raining, and not a morning to be without a nice warm bed. Feeling like I am experimenting on patients like an inept Dr Frankenstein, I decide to make myself useful. I give myself the task of making tea in the large kitchen that also functions as an improvised waiting room. Dr A sets himself up in a corridor off the kitchen and places large posters on the window to give his patients some privacy. I soon have a large pot of tea brewing.

First in is M, who tells me right away, when I ask, that she is depressed. I would also have depression if I were homeless. I handed her a cup of tea. She says, 'Tanks, luv.'

Next in is B, who is very grumpy. He tells me to fuck off. So I do. I go back to pottering around my teapots, but B comes over to investigate. He asks, 'What are you here for? You must be here for something. I don't know what you are here for but you must be here for something.' I am not yet awake enough to explain anthropological methods to him.

The room quickly fills up as I hand round the mugs of hot tea. After a weekend living on the streets, the homeless need something for depression or new dressings for wounds acquired in the battles to survive outside.

A young man in a white tracksuit tells me that Doctor S is 'a prick': 'They send all the trainee doctors up to P_____ St because no one up there seems to have a clue what they are doing. I have been in and out of hospital and none of them know what they are doing. The fuckers threw me out. They are just experimenting on us. Monday morning is fierce busy because we are all here for the scripts.'[13]

M comes back into the kitchen from the improvised surgery. She tells me that Doctor A is a saint.

B gathers an audience for a lecture on his leg. He could be using a PowerPoint projector. 'That's what's killing me,' he says, pointing to a grisly infected knife wound running up his shin. 'One time I had feet that could walk to Kerry on their own. Now ten feet is like climbing Mount Everest. I can't put me foot on the floor. I sat on me bed all day yesterday crying.' He wipes a tear from his grizzled cheek with tattooed fingers that spell H-A-T-E. 'The doctors aren't worried about it, but I am.'

A young girl comes in. I asked her name and she tells me it is Sue. She tells me she is sixteen. I don't believe her because she looks much younger. I ask why she is here. 'I am here for the script. You can't just come down off the methadone suddenly. It is worse than heroin. You can die if you stop. Did you know that? Die!'

'Will you have a cup of tea?' I ask.

'Tanks, pet.'

'Milk?'

'Tanks, just a drop.'

'Sugar?'

'Ten!' She stands, silently mouthing the numbers, as we both count the spoons of sugar going into her tea.

---

[13] Prescriptions for methadone.

6

Business: Enough Cheek for Two Arses

Doing nothing is very hard to do...you never know when you're finished.

(Leslie Nielsen)

Dating back to our earliest historical records, there is evidence that humans, unlike other animals, have engaged in commerce. Work is not unique to us: beavers and ants, amongst others, have reputations for relentless exertion. Commerce is not simply the production of excess to guard against lean times, something which bees do. Our commerce is highly complex and has become a social end in itself. Unlike other animals that work to live, we have developed the live-to-work principle. Our work involves congregating at photocopying machines – which had to be invented for that purpose – and gathering in the pub after a hard day of work avoidance to expend even more energy complaining about the boss.

Different cultures produce variations on business. If you want to be Irish, you should learn how to get into and ultimately succeed in the Irish workplace. After all, this is where the majority of us spend most of our waking hours.

An important means of accessing any culture is to get a job in that culture.

If you can't get a job, try being unemployed because you can learn from that as well. Being unemployed is not a passive state. There are rules governing being on the dole. You have to watch Jeremy Kyle on the telly in the mornings, from bed. Unemployment derives its meaning from work, and vice versa. To maintain this dialectical relationship between the two, you must sustain a connection with work if on the dole. This is usually achieved by applying for jobs. Keep one set of clothes clean in case you get called for interview. When you are not actually wearing these clothes, hang out in the local park in a stained overcoat or lie on the canal bank with your new friends, drinking beer and feeding the ducks and swans.

Attractive as unemployment seems, the shared misery of the workplace also has its attractions for many.

When it comes to researching doing business in Ireland, I don't have to go undercover or engage in traditional participation or observation exercises. I don't even have to persuade an unfortunate captain of industry to give me a job for the sake of social science. Happily, I have a lot of experience in Irish business to draw on. But I have never had a proper job so my experience is not perfect.

* * *

A Proper Job

If you want to be Irish, get yourself what we call a *proper job*. When you get a proper job, you might even have a career. Next to being fired, having a career is the most important thing you can aspire to in the Irish workplace. A career is a proper job with a set rank progression. These ranks should be graded with numbers so that you can easily work out where you are relative to your starting point and your colleagues. To have a successful career, you should concentrate on moving up the numbers and letters, as appropriate. At parties you can tell your fellow revellers that you are a Grade VIIa, Senior P2. Some careers have the happy knack of giving people the title of *senior*. When you are senior, you are entitled to perks: you get to blame the juniors; you also get to say 'I told you so' at management meetings, especially to other seniors.

A proper job is one in which you hope to remain for at least forty years. During those years, you may become an elected politician, complete a prison sentence or be forced to emigrate. But with a proper job, there will always be a desk for you when you are eventually thrown out of office, released early from jail or allowed to return from exile. Your eventual retirement will not be marked by any change in effort. You will simply no longer be required to turn up at the office.

The consoling thing about business is that, even if you don't know what you are doing, it is relatively hard to kill anyone by working in the Sales Department. However, there are barriers to entry to some careers. But remember, you are Irish. Aspire to do what you love rather than what you are good at. For example, if you love singing in the shower and in front of usually polite people, become a popular singer. If you love talking about yourself and your ideas to a captive audience, become a teacher. Your passion should see you through. Sometimes you are required to be qualified, but you will always be asked to send in a CV and, if you are lucky, attend a job interview.

CV Rules

The Curriculum Vitae (CV) purports to document strictly factual information. In Ireland, we are more comfortable with fiction, so you should stick with that genre. Like everyone else, write a fictional CV because it will be more gripping than an account of your actual accomplishments. Furthermore, a CV provides a context in which you are encouraged to write about your positive attributes and achievements. Being Irish, you will naturally find this task difficult because generations of teachers and mammies will have made it impossible for you to write or think anything good about yourself without turning bright red and collapsing into a sweating heap of stammering incoherence. However, to help you achieve this seemingly impossible task, you should use imported business-speak. That was why it was invented.

When using business-speak, remember that you don't have a life, you have *experience*. The first rule of CV writing is to make everything experiential. All previous tasks can be portrayed as experience, which, in turn, should always be described as *valuable*. Despite what you think or have been told by your mammy, you haven't done anything that is a complete waste of time. In business, all experience is counted as positive. All normal human failings must be edited out. Your experience is always *invaluable* or *unique*; your communication is *exceptional*; your leadership is *inspiring* or *innate*; and your dedication to potential employers *unnatural*.

In business-speak there are conventions for describing your miserable life experientially. For example, using a photocopying machine should be described as *managing documents*, which is a valuable skill; making the tea is *catering*, also valuable (who doesn't like a cuppa at work?); answering the phone is being a *communications expert* (where would we be without communications and experts?); and stapling the Christmas party menu together is *making presentations*. Don't be hard on yourself. Drug dealing is *imports and exports* or *sales executive experience*, depending on your position in the gang – which should be described as a *disparate team* presenting *diverse human resource challenges*, which of course you successfully overcame. Safely crossing the road involves *analysing complex vectors and future trajectories* and *implementing appropriate solutions for positive deliverables*. Knowing how to cross the road is a valuable skill. Knowing how to walk and talk at the same time, while crossing the road and looking left and right, is *a set of high value add-on complementary skills designed to produce optimum outcomes*. You weren't a toilet cleaner; you have *supervisory experience of managing small teams under challenging olfactory conditions*, where you were able to *implement dedicated aromatic solutions* by *leveraging available paper-based resources* for *productive outcomes*.

The second rule of CV writing is that gaps in your experience, typically caused by incarceration or years of failed college examinations, should be accounted for by a number of conventional devices. You may write, 'left work for four years for personal reasons.' No one in the context of an Irish interview will ask you about your personal reasons. The panel will be dying to, but they won't ask because nothing is more embarrassing to us than personal information. Claiming to have been in a coma for four years is also acceptable and not at all embarrassing. A surprisingly high number of us have fallen victim to comatose conditions. You should not specify if the coma was drug-induced. Describe your jail time abroad as *voluntary work* in a non-specified overseas location, which covers a great deal. Claiming to have been travelling around Australia is an acceptable CV filler. However, remember that, while one year lost in the outback is *de rigueur*, four years shows a dangerous amount of individualism.

The third rule of CV writing is that you should not list your own interests, which are drinking, avoiding work, eating, staying in bed as long as possible, going home from work as early as possible, daydreaming, staying out late, composing a pocket encyclopaedia of excuses for all occasions or assuming authority without responsibility. Ideally, your interests should be both someone else's and be team-based, with you as the captain. While solitary activities such as reading, cinema, wine tasting, painting, hill walking, cycling, listening to music and writing gothic poetry are all evidence of an unsocial introspection, you might include them because if you do get the job you will be offered a management position.

The fourth rule is that you should nominate eminent people who have only just died as your referees. If no one famous has died recently, current unhappy employers are ideal because they will be delighted to move you on. They will usually agree to write glowingly about your experience and achievements if you promise that you will leave immediately if you get the job. In business this is what is called a *win-win situation*. In any case, if an employer says anything remotely accurate about your general failings, you will be able to prosecute them for defamation on the basis that being 'completely fucking useless' is impossible to prove in court.

Finally, write what you like in your CV, but at the interview, as they say in acting school, *be* that person. Many writers of Irish CVs will simply copy and paste the appropriate jargon on being a self-starting entrepreneur, a motivational leader and speaker, a genius at communications and a management innovator without taking it on board at an existential level – without doing the method training, in other words. It is not uncommon for 'charismatic leaders' to sit in front of interview panels in a catatonic paralysis. As one of my more successful informants told me, 'To make a good impression at an interview, you need enough neck for two heads or enough cheek for a couple of arses.'

Traditionally, Irish people were employed through a recruitment technique known as *pull*. Pull was where one of your relations, already in the organisation, would 'pull you in' by putting pressure on the boss. Persons who were connected to others through kinship, friendship or having intimidating family members who were owed a favour traditionally staffed Irish companies. Because it is impossible to halt the juggernaut of modernising influences, sadly the system of pull has been replaced by the competency-based interview. But if you still value our traditions, get yourself pulled into a job because it will spare you developing your interview techniques. Tell your mother that you are going to work with her tomorrow. If all your relations are unemployed, send out a hundred custom-written CVs to a wide variety of companies. Sit back and wait for the interview.

Interviews: The Self-Depreciation Rule

During the course of your interview, you will inevitably be asked about your weaknesses. If you are honest, you will get the job. If you lie by describing your weaknesses as being on a slide towards alcoholism; blogging all day on your laptop; not liking to get up out of bed before 11.30 a.m.; not liking to make decisions or take responsibility; and being happiest while daydreaming of a different life in a tropical country, you shouldn't expect to get the job. What your potential employer is looking for is honesty, so you should tell the truth. The truth is that, if anything, you are too conscientious; you take on more work than is good for you; you have no home life so you like to work late into the evening; your motivation goes way beyond being paid; you like to take on responsibility without any authority; and you are happiest while taking on extra work. If you have one really big weakness, it is trying to do the work of five people. Such honesty will get you the job.

The First Day Rule – Exhibiting Enthusiasm

On the morning of your first day in your new job, you should plan for your retirement. Meet your pension representative to make sure that your payments will be in place so that you can retire as soon as possible. But before that happy day comes, you have to settle into work. Conventionally, it is important to make a good impression on your first morning. Work etiquette demands that you not be more than fifteen minutes late. While it is acceptable to look happy on your first day, thereafter you should exhibit as many symptoms of clinical depression as possible and participate in the communal complaining.

Appearing happy at work is a breach of work protocol. Your boss will become anxious if you look happy. He may start to worry that you know something he doesn't. Maybe you are planning to leave for a better job. It's not that he cares about you; it's just that he doesn't want you to be happy somewhere else. 'Employees these days', he is likely to think, 'You just can't get good ones. Not like in the old days when we were all happy to be miserable together head-butting rocks in the quarry.' Use *Peig* as your role model. Remember how unhappy Peig was working in that shop in Dingle and how she didn't complain about it more than nineteen times per day. Therefore, even if you are not miserable, you should act and look miserable from your second day onwards because you don't want to upset the boss. This is particularly important if you are a receptionist. Following sporadic feelings of guilt, because you look so miserable, your boss will attempt to cheer you up with small bonuses. In general, looking depressed is the quickest and most effective way of giving the impression that you are hardworking and efficient.

On the first day, you may be taken around to meet your colleagues, who will be introduced as your teammates.

Don't try to get on with them; try to bond with them. Don't have arguments with them; have diverging strategies. Don't have bitching sessions; have team meetings. If there is a welcome lunch, go to it and stay at it all afternoon drinking the complementary wine. Go from there to the after-work drinks session. Make sure that you start a drunken brawl with your teammates. This will mean that you will be too unwell to come in to work for your second day. Result!

The Rules of Taking Sickies

If you do manage to drag yourself in on the second day, use your time to fill in your leave sheet. The normal working week runs from Monday to Friday, inclusive. However, traditionally you can take Mondays as a sickie along with your allotted holidays and Bank Holidays. As no one can do anything on a Friday afternoon, there is no point in coming back into the office after lunch on a Friday. If you take a day of your holidays each week, say, Tuesdays, you can average a two-and-a-half-day week. Make sure to come in on Friday mornings because they are a doss anyway. You can still take two weeks' holidays during the summer by contracting some kind of resistant virus.

You should inform your new employer as soon as possible of your disabling conditions. Something that keeps coming back, which is both incurable and embarrassing, will cover your Mondays. Parasites are unfairly maligned. In the right host, they have their uses. Parasites growing somewhere inside you are good. You can bring pictures to the office. A parasite that becomes active after Sunday lunch is even better because it can be 'playing havoc' with your kidneys by Monday. Escape-artist parasites are best as these can evade the weekly attempts at the hospital to evict them from your chosen organ. A parasite with a large number of bene-ficiaries is an attractive choice because these can take over

119

in the unlikely event of a successful eviction of the parasite. Anything that prevents your employers enquiring too closely is good. For instance, piles. You can bring photos of these into the canteen. People will stop asking. But remember not to look like you enjoy sitting down, even though you do it quite often. Squirm in your chair every now and again for effect, especially if asked at a meeting to make a decision.

You can also have a large family of disease-prone relations at home, who you are obliged to rush to the hospital at least once a week, preferably on Mondays. Why not let the whole family be hosts to a parasite you all picked up at a salad bar in Morocco? Remember, you can only have your appendix out twice because surgeons have been known to leave a teensy-weensy bit behind the first time. In order to avoid the attention of *The Lancet* journal, you can donate only one kidney to a sibling, but you can be the recipient of as many as you like. On the morning a colleague of mine was due back at work after she set a new world record for the length of time needed to recover from an appendectomy, her husband fell down the stairs and concussed himself. Nice one!

As a male employee, you can ask for maternity leave for your phantom pregnancy. What employer wants to see that go to the Labour Court?

Don't waste the benefits of a real disease. If you are actually sick, go to work to show the suppurating lesions in your armpits to your boss. When he pays for the taxi to take you home, you have the satisfaction of knowing he won't want you back any time soon.

How to Be Important

It is practically impossible to understand who is in charge of things at work and who has the power. There are three fundamental laws of power in the Irish workplace. The first states that the less important you actually are, the more effort you invest in convincing your colleagues that you are actually important. The corollary of this is also true – the more important your colleagues come to think you might be, the less important you have actually become. The second law of power states that if you really are important you are less likely to try to convince anyone of your importance. However, if you don't try to convince people of your importance, the less important you will become. The third law states that most people are not important to the organisation. If you actually are important, it is unlikely that you will think you are not. Therefore, it follows that those who try to look important are not, and those who don't try probably are, unless they actually are not important. The most confusing group are those who are not important but feel they should be.

This means that when you turn up for work on your first day, it is impossible to tell who really is important and who you can ignore, because most of the unimportant are masquerading as essential to the company. The important are probably cleaning the toilets as the ultimate demonstration of their hidden powers. How can you tell the difference? It is not necessary. Just join in and try to look important. Helpfully, there are a few rules you can follow.

The Size-of-Office Rule

Genuinely powerful people within your organisation may have enormous offices. But, then, so also may losers. You will need to carefully study the details to work out who is who. These offices will be decorated with hardwoods, preferably mahogany, with matching billiard-table-sized desks. It is crucial to put some thought into the type of wood used for panelling so as not to make the wrong impression. As a general rule, don't use an endangered species of tree unless you advertise it to everyone. A genuinely important boss should be willing to reinforce their ruthlessness symbolically. A white rhinoceros skin on the floor and an ashtray made from a mountain gorilla hand will impress. But for the aspiring middle manager with less means, the presence of a dead plant will also signify authority. The dead plant will connote that this person is too busy to properly look after it; watch out, because if he neglects a plant, you may be next. But appearances can be deceiving. Anyone who goes to the trouble of bringing a dead plant into work to instil fear in their employees is not worth fearing. If they are really important, they would have a lackey just to water the plants. You should fear the big office with the jungle running along one wall hiding the full-time gardener. Don't fear the office with all the files piled up on the desk in the lame attempt to give the impression of frantic work. Everyone knows that the higher up the scale you are, the less work you have to do.

Inversely, there is the one-of-the-lads boss who occupies the smallest and darkest office because she leads from the back. She may actually be in control or she may just have issues with asserting her authority. Like the boss with the big office, it is unwise to form a rash judgement on the basis of first appearances. Look for the small clues. I once had a boss who condescended to occupy a small office only because she went on a management course where she was persuaded that it was better to look like she was one of the lads. She wasn't a great student, so, while she moved to a smaller office, she brought her Alessi limited-edition tea set with her. Also, her hair gave her away because she had power-hair to match her power suits. Watch out for the woman in the Paul Costelloe suit in the tiny office.

Then there is the boss who is so important that he has no office at all. He will turn up some morning asking, 'Do you mind if I borrow a corner of your desk for a minute?' Before you can say no, he will have sat down, opened his laptop and proceeded to use your phone to confirm his afternoon golf partners. Then he will confide that he has to prepare a short presentation for the Chairman of the Board. He will say, 'Oh, but that's me. What the hell am I presenting to myself for? [Laughing manically] Sorry for disturbing you.' He will then leave. If anyone occupies a corner of your desk, wait about ten seconds, look at your watch and then exclaim, 'My God is that the time! I am late for a meeting.' Then run away.

Title Rules

We have a national weakness for bureaucracy and those who tell you that they have no interest in it are the worst offenders. The best way to express your bureaucratic self is through your title. When you have kitted out your office to an appropriate standard of intimidation, you need to think about the title that will appear on your nameplate on the door. If you are an anarchist, just put your name on the door. If not, you need a title to signify your place within the organisation. It is not conventional to call yourself *Lord of the Universe, King of All You See* or just plain *The Boss of You*. You have to follow the rules of titles. Fortunately, the rule governing assigning titles is time consuming and, if you are the boss, will give you something useful to do when you do turn up at work.

First, divide the company into arbitrary departments. For each haphazard department, start at the bottom and, as you work your way up, make each title longer and more abstract than the one below. For example, in your Administration Department (God, don't ask what they do!) call the people at the bottom *Assistants*. These, who have neither doors nor nameplates, can be herded together in open plan offices. They report to the *Administration Assistant Officers* who have desks in the open plan office that either face the wall or the windows, if you actually have windows in the cellar (some employers really spoil their staff). The Administrative Assistant Officers report to the *Heads of Administrative Assistant Development*, who can have glass cubicles in the corner of the cellar. You may fit in four of these for symmetry. This will be the level at which employees will be allowed a title plate on the side of the cubicle.

As you will now be running out of room on your title plates, you can drop back to shorter titles by the device of introducing the term *Supervisor*. This allows you to start again, working your way up following the same principles. Down the hall, in a two-per-office set-up, you should have the *Administration Supervisors*. In the first office, we find the *Supervisor of Administration*, who reports to the *Administration Supervisor Officers*, who in turn report to the *Heads of Administration Supervisor Officers*. Ideally, you should have as many of the latter as you can afford, to facilitate the distribution of blame, undermine clear reporting lines, divorce responsibility from authority and sow confusion. The responsibility of the Heads of Administrative Supervisor Officers is to make sure that no one ever works out what exactly is happening in Administration.

Upstairs, with access to natural light, you should have the offices of those to whom the ones in the cellar report. Including the term *Director* in their title can indicate their superior status. In their own office, but without windows, you should have at least two *Directors of Administration Supervisors*. In the next office, with a paint-on window, we find the *Director of the Supervisor of Administration*, who reports to the *Director of Administration Supervisor Officer*, who has a window that doesn't open. This person, in turn, reports to the *Directors of the Heads of Administration Supervisor Officers*. Again, have as many of these as possible, but allow them to have windows.

Repeat this process as you go up from floor to floor, introducing the terms *Senior, Director of Development* and

Vice-President. This structure can be reproduced for each of your random departments by substituting the words *Human Resources, Engineering, Sales, Marketing, Quality Assurance, Research & Development*, etc. in the place of *Administration*. The only occasion on which a member of one department should communicate with a member of a different department is if there is a fire in the building, and only then after an agreement has been reached by the joint heads of supervision for those departments affected by the blaze. In general, in the case of fire, the people in the cellar can stay where they are. If you have five departments, for example, ideally you should have five departmental vice-presidents. If any employee becomes unhappy, you should agree to include the terms *Joint, Vice, Chief, Senior, Function, Executive, Regional, Divisional, Transnational* or *Chancellor* in their title, as you see fit on the day. Finally, on the top floor is the *President*, which is you. Get yourself a white Persian cat.

Punctuality Rules

Even if you are not the President, another way of demonstrating your own self-importance in the Irish workplace is by the punctuality rule. The later you turn up to meetings, the more important you clearly are. If you don't turn up at all, it's obviously because you are very important. Always arrive late for meetings. When you get there, offer the apology that you were tied up at an even more important meeting than the one currently underway. As a bookend to this, try to anticipate the right moment during the meeting to jump to your feet shouting, 'Oh, I am late for an important meeting,' and run out of the room, thereby demonstrating your condescension to have been present at all. It is difficult to get the timing exactly right. Don't leave too soon, but don't allow yourself to be upstaged by another important person at the meeting. For this reason, meetings can be very stressful.

Phone Etiquette

Another rule is that the more phone calls you receive, the more important you are. Hire someone to continuously ring you on your mobile. If your budget doesn't stretch to this, set the alarm on your phone to ring every few minutes. Pretend someone is on the other end. Immediately following your profuse and intentionally hammy apology for being late for a meeting – because you really don't want anyone to get the impression that you actually care – your phone should ring. You should say, 'Oh, it's you. I am sorry I can't talk right now because I am at an important meeting. Can I ring you back? Really? Really? What did he say to that? What did you say? How did you leave it?' At this point, place your hand over the phone and whisper confidentially to everyone at the meeting that you are really sorry but that you just have to take this call because it is really important. Proceed to talk loudly, preferably with shouts and threats, for at least ten minutes without leaving the meeting. When you finish, say – again, with the least conviction you can manage – 'Sorry about that. Where were we?' At this point, your phone should ring again. Roll your eyes, as if saying 'What can you do?' Answer the phone and repeat the routine above. You should do this at least three times per meeting.

For advanced phone etiquette, you need two mobile phones that are connected by speed dial. Hide one phone in your pocket or handbag. Leave the other on your desk. When one of your minions comes to your office to ask a tricky question such as 'Have you read the report I sent you that you screamed at me last week to write, which took me sixty hours to do over the weekend?', hit the speed-dial button on your hidden mobile. When the mobile on your desk rings, hold up a finger to halt the diatribe of the underling, while debating aloud with yourself why you cannot talk right now. Keep this drama going until your employee leaves the office.

If you have a particularly contrary employee before you, pause the phone 'conversation' and say, 'Is it okay if I get back to you because I just have to deal with this important phone call right now?' Repeat this tactic on every occasion that an employee comes to your office looking for feedback, because it is more productive than actually reading a report. This approach is especially useful for anyone with a financial role who deals daily with irritating employees looking for pay reviews, invoices to be paid, equipment, holidays or leave, paper or paper-clips, or those who are informing you that the building is on fire.

E-mailing Etiquette

Technology has transformed the way in which we work. For example, computer technology allows many of us to work from home or even to work all night after we get home. Smart phones and e-mails allow us to maintain constant contact with the office in case there are any vital business developments or essential office gossip, even while we sleep.

There are rules about what you should do when writing and sending company e-mails. First, never use the subject heading because it is unhelpful for your recipient to know what the e-mail is about. Second, always write your e-mail while drunk after lunch. Third, write stuff that you only want the recipient to read, so make it as personal as possible. The idea that the Director of the Heads of Technical Supervisors has access to all e-mails on the server is just an office myth put about by the self-important Technical Department. The belief round the office that the boss has access to all e-mails is just a technological impossibility. I just don't believe it. Make sure that your title on the e-mail signature is accurate and up-to-date. Put your e-mails on a timer to send between 11.00 p.m. and 4.00 a.m., giving the recipient the impression that you were in the office all night. Finally, don't open, answer or acknowledge e-mails that purport to be important. Helpfully, the number of red exclamation marks indicates the degree of importance of the e-mail.

It is accepted in psychiatry that if someone writes to you in capitalised green font they are criminally insane. If you receive such an e-mail, you should leave the building immediately.

How to Be Stressed

Promotion is generally confined to those managers who have demonstrated no capacity for dealing with stress. If you really care about your work, you shouldn't be able to cope. The ideal is to die from a burst blood vessel two rungs from the top of the company ladder. You will be guaranteed a company funeral where your employees will do their best to pretend that they are unhappy that you are dead (it's in their contract).

There are several well-established ways of demonstrating an inability to cope with stress. By sticking with these you can be confident of winning the recognition of those above you.

Carrying out acts in a logical sequence is an indication that you are managing a project well. You could try starting at the end and working backwards. Shredding cheques as they come into the accounts office is also good. Talk to yourself or mutter as you hurry down the corridors. Try to be perpetually red in the face. I used to work with someone who spent all of his time, when he wasn't attacking his colleagues, apologising to them because he was so stressed. Cool!

But the best way to show that you are stressed is to be a control freak. If you can't do your job, do someone else's. Better still, do everyone else's. As most of us in Ireland cannot handle our own responsibilities, because of our cultural fatalism, we are more comfortable taking on the problems of others. There are more control freaks per square metre of carpet tiles in Ireland than anywhere else in the world.

My management superhero idol is the control-freak micro-manager. I find that the most satisfying form of micro-management is changing the toilet rolls in all of the toilets in a secret sequence that you can work out in advance. Start in the women's toilet in the cellar and work your way up. Next day, you can start with the men's. The following day, you can work your way from the top down. After that, there is the possibility of starting at the first floor, and so on. The permutations are endless and it is much more satisfying than writing the business plan for the next shareholders AGM.

Boardroom Rules

Anthropologists know that the language we use is a vital element in producing group identity. Business, and management in particular, relies heavily on adapting metaphors to the workplace. The most effective metaphors are sporting, nautical and, if under fire, military. If you want to be accepted into the elite group comprising the members of the board, you have to perfect your metaphors. Never refer to your business as an actual business – refer to it as a vessel. In order to mark your coming on board or to avoid being hoisted by your own petard or to prevent the vessel being holed below the waterline, you will be encouraged to paddle your own canoe and put your back to the oar, unless you feel you have to pass the baton. When things get really bad because there is a storm brewing and your comrades are under fire because they have missed the starting gun, it will be all hands on deck. Eventually, after you have manned the pumps, you will be asked to take one for the team because you were flying the flag. Ask the sales people to storm the barriers and to dig deep because they have been playing below par. There is no future, only *going forward*. You will get nothing done but, with a favourable wind behind you, you may win the day.

Some of us are like gofers that like to burrow into issues while some of us are more weevil-like, drilling down into issues until we bottom out.

The Rules of Resolving Disputes

Anthropologists find it useful to deal with the complex issue of disputes and conflict resolution through case studies, where a selection of disparate examples can illustrate the issues in their real contexts. The Irish workplace is filled with disputes. This is another reason why it is of interest to anthropology. In general, Irish managers hate confrontation. A boss will do almost anything to avoid a scene. Therefore, only the most extraordinary circumstances will result in your being called into the office for a reprimand. A typical example would be failure to turn up for work for six months or knocking a colleague down with your car while they were standing at the photocopier. But if it does come to a show-down, you should keep it personal. This will be to your advantage because the boss will have just read his *Guide to Good Management* book, which will have advised him not to make it personal. A typical scenario that I was frequently involved in went as follows:

> Me [sitting at my huge mahogany desk with three living plants – work that out!]: Oh, yeah. Come in. Sit down. I, ah, wanted to talk to you about something [embarrassed mutterings about attempted murder].
> Intractable Employee: Did you see the match last night? Liverpool won. They are your team, aren't they?

Me: No, they are not. Let's stick to the subject at hand. Look, this isn't easy for me but I have to tell you that I am not happy with your performance.

Intractable Employee: Oh, that's surprising because I thought you looked like a Liverpool fan!

Me: What is that supposed to mean?

Intractable Employee: Never mind. What's this perform-ance? Are we in a play now? I haven't been well. I have been diagnosed with Parkinson's disease. Look at the shake in my hand.

Me: I have to fire you.

Intractable Employee: You can't fire me. You have to give me a verbal warning followed by a written warning and then you can fire me.

Me: I have already given you a verbal warning.

Intractable Employee: You haven't.

Me: I have.

[Repeat this exchange ten times.]

Intractable Employee: Liar. You didn't.

Me: I did, but to be sure I am giving you another one now.

Intractable Employee: Okay. So was there anything else? I need to get out of this office. I am allergic to polyester carpets.

Me: Now you can go, but I need you to improve your performance at work. The whole building is covered with this carpet.

Intractable Employee [scratching]: No wonder I can't stop itching every time I come into work. I must look into compensation. I won't be in tomorrow because I am over at the hospital having an MRI scan.

Me: Didn't you have an MRI last week?

Intractable Employee [sighing]: That was for something else. Christ, what a Nazi. Look at the shake in that hand.

[Intractable Employee leaves the office, making small talk with his colleagues on his way out of the building.]

To illustrate conflict in the Irish work environment, I have selected two cases. For *The Strange Case of Wrongful Dismissal*, I went to the Labour Court to witness proceedings. For *The Mysterious Case of 'the Deposit' on the Canteen Table*, I relied on eyewitness testimony, which anthropology treats as scientifically reliable.

The Strange Case of Wrongful Dismissal

Once I was asked to be a character witness in a dispute at the Labour Court. A junior fired a colleague for challenging her authority. She said, 'How dare you question my authority. You are fired.' Because he had very little experience of the workplace, astonishingly, the employee packed up his belongings and left. Eventually, he was in court claiming compensation for unfair dismissal because, as he said, he 'hadn't done anything wrong'. I thought that this was an open-and-shut case until the company produced a very expensive defence barrister. This barrister called our boss of bosses to the witness stand and began to question him in the following way:

> Barrister: Are you the boss?
> Boss: Yes, I am.
> Barrister: What kind of a boss would you say you are?
> Boss: I would describe myself as lacking both authority and competence.
> Barrister: In other words, you don't know what you are doing.
> Boss: That is correct.
> Barrister: How would you describe anyone who obeyed your orders?
> Boss: I would say that they were an idiot.
> Barrister: Would it then be fair to say – don't look at him, look at me – that anyone who obeys your orders or the orders of anyone who works for you is an idiot?

Boss: Yes. That would be fair.

Barrister: So, if anyone in your company was fired by either you or anyone authorised by you, what should they do?

Boss: They should just go about their normal business.

Barrister: Go about their normal business [nods, repeating this twice for effect]. Thank you, boss of bosses. You may step down. [Addressing the gallery] Your Honour, I put it to you that this employee connived in his own wilful removal from work. Just because he was told by this self-confessed idiot or his representative idiots that he was fired, he left the workplace and went home [snorts in distain]. He should have ignored those fools and carried on regardless. He should have waited until he was removed from the building by unreasonable force. His claim for unfair dismissal should be dismissed.

It was!

The moral of this tale is, in the extraordinary event that you are actually fired, chain yourself to your desk and wait to be thrown out with disproportionate force.

The Mysterious Case of 'the Deposit' on the Canteen Table

An informant told me about a disturbance at his place of work, which was a large architectural firm. Just before lunch, an employee shat[14] on a table in the small staff canteen. The collective olfactory senses of the queue of architects strolling in for lunch were overwhelmed by the stench of the fresh steaming turd on the table nearest the ban marie containing the Special of the Day. Their appetites were instantly destroyed, so they stampeded back to their desks gagging and gasping for air. With the help of a private detective, the boss quickly determined that the offending act took place

---

[14] Hiberno-English – past tense of *to shit*.

just minutes before the official lunch break. However, this deduction did not help him to draw up a list of suspects. But he wasn't the boss for nothing. He made it known by e-mail that he would be carrying out DNA testing on all staff for comparison with the DNA already taken from 'the deposit'. Knowing that the game was up, the offender surrendered himself. Just before giving himself up, he destroyed a scale model on display in the lobby with a hammer. He offered as an excuse for his behaviour his inability to deal with stress. He was promoted a few weeks later.

* * *

During an extended anthropological trip to Poland, I got a special present from a very powerful and successful former communist woman with occult powers. One day, this woman presented me with a small coffin-shaped wooden box that contained what she described as a magical tie. Lifting the lid, I saw, lying like a corpse on a bed of satin, a battered and stained bright red tie with a pattern of over-sized blue elephants; the kind of tie to take seriously. She told me that the tie, which belonged to her father, would guarantee a very happy outcome if I wore it to a job inter-view. Some people wear school ties to interviews; I have my magic tie.

Within a few weeks, I had an opportunity to try out my tie at an academic interview. I flew half way across the world for the interview, to which I wore my best suit, a new shirt and my magical tie, so that the elephants grinned across the desk at the interview panel. I didn't get the job.

Once back in Poland, I complained bitterly that it was not a lucky tie but just a stinking rag that was never going to get me a job. The woman who gave it to me wisely explained that she never said that the tie would get me a job; she also said that I obviously had a lucky outcome at my interview.

If, like me, you have a lucky tie, leave it in your drawer when going to a job interview because very few of us actually want what is good for us. Getting a job that you like would take all the fun out of work.

7

Building: Have You Seen My Tec-7?

When one has finished building one's house, one suddenly realizes that in the process one has learned something that one really needed to know in the worst way – before one began.

(Friedrich Nietzsche)

Archaeology is the branch of anthropology that studies the remnants of past cultures. Ruins are usually the only things that endure from otherwise lost civilizations. These remains are mostly ancient buildings, both the palaces and castles of the powerful and the humble dwellings of the peasants. But archaeology cannot tell us about the attitudes and behaviours of those who originally constructed these buildings. By studying the behaviour of those we hire to put up our house extensions, which are the ruins of the future, we can get some insight into ancient building behaviour, because builders follow long-established habits. The study of Irish builders is a variation on archaeology in that it provides an insight into the nature of our future precious archaeological relics.

From an anthropological point of view, builders are also an important source of Irishness. Being a builder is one of the most common occupations in Irish life. We have travelled the world as builders. Most of us have a relationship with builders because of our close connections with our houses. In our dealings with builders, we encounter our innermost being.

Ironically, the property crash in Ireland has brought us into closer contact with builders than at any time during the Celtic Tiger. In the past, when it was impossible to contemplate living any longer with that lime-green colour in the spare bedroom or the kitchen worktop that was absolutely the wrong variety of hardwood, there was no alternative but to find a new house. After a couple of years living with those plaid curtains it was time to move on again. All of this was done at the expense of accumulating bigger and bigger mortgages. The scarcity of credit has made this kind of movement away from the offending décor impossible. Thus, this economic crisis has created an outbreak of house renovations. Instead of fleeing our houses in removal vans in the dead of night, we have started to renovate them. We can actually contemplate painting that bedroom, changing that worktop and, while we are at it, building on extra spaces. In England, one's house is one's home. In Ireland, one's house is one's house. Once it has been perfected it can become a home, but not before perfection has been achieved, and perfection is always a roll of wallpaper away.

When both our properties and our property markets collapse, we get the builders in. We also get them in to stick extensions on to the back or sides of our houses that dwarf the original structures. We need huge kitchens to facilitate more eating-in; spacious playrooms that can be used by family members of all ages wielding Wii batons; and – the high point of renovations – the attic bedroom for our smaller family members.

Would anyone revamp their house just for research? I would. But fortunately I didn't have to because I was renovating anyway. I, too, am seeking perfection. If you really want to be Irish, build an extension on to your house using Irish builders.

As an added benefit we might even learn how to become builders ourselves. If you are an aspiring DIY guru, you may find the rules governing builder behaviour a useful practical guide. No matter how stressed you become, you should remember your responsibility to the greater project. Imagine future archaeologists scratching their heads in five thousand years time as they uncover your unique kitchen–diner, speculating that it must have had ritual significance because it doesn't look practical to them.

* * *

We Irish are famous, especially in England, for being builders, specifically labourers. Our reputation does not lie in designing famous buildings, but in the labour that goes into them. If we had built the pyramids, we would not have been the architects, the Egyptians; we would have been the Israelites. We would have provided the manpower. Besides being internationally famous as labourers, we are also obsessed with house ownership. We would rather own our own hovel than rent a palace. Our obsession with house ownership may be a consequence of our historical lack of possession of the country in general. If our houses are our most precious possessions, then our connection with those we allow to tear them apart and put them back together again is as important as our relationship with our doctors when we find ourselves in hospital for major surgery.

I won't be paying attention to the quality of our buildings. Neither am I particularly concerned with what is being built, nor the technical aspects of building, such as the tools, materials and regulations. I am interested in how surviving an encounter with a builder can tell us something about being Irish. Although we don't have to worry about building techniques, we should take into account that there are carpenters, plumbers, electricians, plasterers, bricklayers, etc., all of whose particular trade-related rules should be noted as variations on a general building theme. By the way, I was able to find a builder, Phil, by carefully following the rules outlined below. I was lucky because Phil is not just a very decent builder, he also helped me with my research. I also learned about *Tec-7* from Phil. Tec-7 is the very latest wonder in building technology. It is a glue, bonder and filler. It is also probably nourishing when spread on your sandwiches. It is all you need to hold your entire house together. If it has a hidden flaw, it will definitely be responsible for many future ruins.

From an anthropological point of view, of course, I was curious about the fact that we have popular nicknames for some types of tradesmen, but not for others. For example, we know bricklayers are *brickies*; carpenters are *chippies*; and electricians are *sparks*. But what about plumbers, painters and plasterers? Phil enlightened me. Plasterers are called *The Spread*, which seems bizarre. Yes, I get it. They spread plaster. Painters are informally known to their fellows as *piss artists* because, from a builder's point of view, 'If you can piss, you can paint.' I think this insult probably reveals an innate insecurity builders have for the more creative aspects of a project. Also, painters have to hide the mistakes of the others as best they can, especially those of The Spread. Tec-7 really helps the piss artists. Plumbers are known as *plumbers*, which, Phil believes, probably comes from the Latin *plumbum* for lead. Maybe plumbing is just boring.

Builder Types

The rules come into effect when you try to find a builder. You are likely to come upon two varieties of builder: *decent* and *cowboy* builders. You are looking for a decent builder. This is the term used by experienced renovators. It is common for one's neighbours to tell you that they had a decent builder in the house just last week or that their cousin is actually a decent builder. Decent builders are the type we recommend to each other. They are the opposite of cowboys, who are to be avoided at all costs. However, this is where it gets tricky. Cowboys are adept at passing themselves off as decent builders: they disguise themselves as decent builders. In fact, that is where they apply most of their energy. A decent builder can become a cowboy during the course of a job. The transformation of a decent builder into a cowboy seems to be a one-way process, because there is no evidence that a cowboy ever became decent during a build.

Decent and cowboy builders behave in exactly the same way. You might suspect that what distinguishes them is their behaviour. It isn't. Obviously cowboy builders may cause you more stress, but there is only one significant difference between the two. Your building will fall down if a cowboy builds it. How, I hear you ask in horror, can you be sure you are not hiring a cowboy? How can you be confident your new roof won't blow off in the first winter storm? You can't be. One way you can tell is to wait six months to see what happens to your neighbour's new extension. You should probably wait a year or maybe eighteen months, or more, just to be sure.

One of my neighbours was willing to relate her experiences with a cowboy builder after I plied her with three gin and tonics. Extraordinary age, combined with the alcohol, made her philosophical. She was having her attic converted as an extra bedroom for her great-grandchildren when they visited at the weekends. The attic ceiling would be low, she told me, but that was okay because her great-grandchildren were still small. By the time they grow tall, they won't visit or she will have 'kicked the bucket' anyway. She hired someone who came highly recommended as a decent builder by her home help. She told me that she had been told the builder had 'done a great job on the attic' of the home help's sister's house. This is typical of the way recommendations make their way through a locality.

My neighbour has a new hip. During the build, the attic bedroom was accessible only by a steep ladder, so she was reluctant to climb up for regular checks on progress. However, after more than a week of worrying and listening to hammering from above, she climbed up very slowly, gingerly alighting onto what she considered to be a very flimsy-looking floor. The builder was crouched under the eaves doodling with something. She asked him to confirm that the floor was sufficiently robust to hold her great-grandchildren. Indignant, the builder took up a position under the roofline where he had maximum head room. Still crouching, he jumped up and down to demonstrate that the floor was, in his own words, 'as solid as a rock, luv'. He then promptly disappeared from view through the floor into the room below. My neighbour made her way back down the ladder as quickly as she could to discover that the builder had bounced off the bed, which broke his fall, and now lay face-down on the floor. When she checked to see if he was still alive, he informed her, from his horizontal viewing point, that her 'skirting boards need replacing, luv'. This is one of many examples of a decent builder transforming into a cowboy at an indeterminate point during a building project.

Building Myths

Anthropologists are interested in the role of myths in a community. There are plenty of myths relating to builders to keep us interested. We call them *myths*; you might call it just being stupid. Most myths promote the idea that cowboy and decent builders are easily distinguishable from each other. In reality they are not. According to one local myth, only cowboy builders travel round in big flashy vans advertising their skills and ideal projects. Supposedly, decent builders prefer anonymous battered vans. This myth probably has its origins in the hope, rather than the reality, that people in battered vans are modest in both character and charges. Another myth has it that decent builders do not park on the footpaths, nor do they cause noise at any time during the building project. These are the exclusive behaviours of cowboys. Furthermore, they don't produce clouds of dust that hang above your roof as if an atom bomb has been detonated in your garden shed. Nor, supposedly, do they demolish the main pipe supplying water to the entire street. Both decent and cowboy builders regularly do those sorts of thing when working on house extensions.

Another myth expounds the advantages of direct labour. In this scenario, you should not hire a building contractor at all but instead go the direct-labour route, where you, as project manager, hire each tradesman directly yourself. Direct labour always seems like a good idea at the very beginning of a project. However, it simply means that, instead of searching for one builder, you have to search for a number of tradesmen. The rules of building still apply. You will end up applying them over and over again, while failing to learn from the experience because of the amnesia rule discussed below. You will increase tenfold the potential for hiring cowboys and combinations of cowboys. Don't do it! While you may save money, you will end up in a lunatic asylum.

The most common myth relates to the belief that a decent builder will not follow the rules of the skip. The view on skips is that cowboy builders will always place the skip on the part of your street that maximises the potential inconvenience to the largest number of neighbours and public service providers. The location will be selected after much careful research, followed by trial and error. Some of my neighbours believe that cowboys even engage in overnight stakeouts of potential skip sites.

A cowboy will position your skip to maximise the number of blocked driveways. On his instruction, the skip-hire company will deliver the skip at twilight, facilitating your neighbours sneaking out under the cover of darkness loaded with old carpets, mattresses and any other bulky items that we keep in our sheds just for such occasions. By dawn, the skip will be filled to overflowing. Your cowboy builder will tell you that this is the reason why he cannot move the mini-mountain of rubble, now growing outside what is left of your kitchen window. Of course, you have to contact the skip-hire company yourself, as your builder has to leave to buy a uniquely shaped shovel for your uniquely shaped debris.

When dealing with builders, it helps if you have something in common. It's good if you can hammer a nail into a piece of two-by-four. If you don't know what two-by-four is then you are the ideal client that the cowboy builder is out there searching for. Remember, as you search for that decent builder, that cowboy builder is searching for you – the supremely gullible client.

Building Rules

Builders refer to what they do as *the building game*. The Austrian philosopher Ludwig Wittgenstein developed the concept of a language game to explain the rules of ordinary conversations. He believed that language was like a game. Games take a wide variety of forms, such as those that can be played alone, with a partner or as part of a team, etc. Each game has its own complex set of rules that must be learned in order to play. Interestingly, Wittgenstein thought that you only really knew the rules of any game when you understood how to break those rules and – hopefully – not get caught. For Wittgenstein, the notion of the game is not just about language: it is a metaphor for life. Irish builders know, probably since before Wittgenstein, that building is a game in all its glorious convolutions. They know how to play. The best builders know all the rules and how to break them. There are a few general rules you should keep in mind if you want to find a builder and play the building game.

Finding a Builder – The Word-of-Mouth Rule

If you are a complete novice, you will try to find your builder in the *Golden Pages*. When you ring up, the builder will ask how you heard of him in order to check your gullibility quotient. When you reply that you found him in the Golden Pages, you are immediately in trouble because he now knows that you are clueless. Only novices hire AAAA Aardvark Builders.

Decent builders are not found in the phonebook. Start your search for a decent builder locally. There will always be a renovation going on somewhere in your neighbourhood. Find a newly completed local extension and keep an eye on it for at least six months after the builders have finally left. Make sure that the job has not just slowed down to a point where, because there hasn't been a builder on site for a month, you imagine it must be finished. Experience, which you won't have at this stage, would teach you to recognise the many tactics builders adopt to abandon your job for any other. Builders will leave ladders propped against gable walls, tools piled in mounds on the sitting-room floor and cement mixers in driveways as territorial markers. Erect scaffolding is particularly good at giving the impression that the builder will be back soon. So wait until all such signs are gone.

Apart from the close study of completed projects, decent builders are usually sourced through word-of-mouth. You can begin by making polite enquiries of your neighbours. This is socially productive because you have to participate in the ritualised exchange of building-related lurid anecdotes that are an integral part of the experience. If you haven't any anecdotes to exchange – because you are a renovation virgin – confine yourself to sympathetic mutterings and appropriate consoling noises, such as: 'Oh, you poor thing'; 'That's awful. How did you cope?'; 'How could you stand it?; or 'Where did ye go after the kitchen burned down?'

As soon as any building work starts in your parish, neighbourhood or street, go directly to that house to solicit information on how the builder was sourced; what jobs he finished and when; and what part of the country he is from. Apart from just interrogating your neighbour, you should also offer comfort in the form of hopeful sentiments, such as, 'Yes, Cavan builders are supposed to be good.' You should at least show some interest in your neighbour's current emotional state. It is usual to invite those who have secured a builder around to your own house for a tea or coffee to 'get away from the mess'. Once they are through the door, you can grill them further.

The Dress Code

Before inviting a prospective builder into your own house, you should remove any evidence of exotic, eccentric or expensive taste that will be read as vulnerability by the builder. Think of it as a first date. His impressions will allow him to gauge how much he can charge for the job on top of any material costs proposed in the project. Present yourself as conservatively as possible, especially in the matter of money. An appropriate sartorial presentation is vital. Dress to appear practical. Dress to look like you know what you are doing. You should not wear actual overalls. Sixties-style dungarees matched with plaid shirts, denim and wool all connote a relationship with manual labour, however abstract. You could dab paint onto visible skin. Borrow well-worn tools from your friends or neighbours and leave them lying around in plain view, not on the polished side-board but casually leaning in a corner, for example. You could leave them on the mantlepiece, emulating standard builder habits. You could roughen both sides of your hands with fine-grain sandpaper. I think P120 is best but I am not sure. Experiment. You should not wear silk or a suit unless it is of matching denim. The rule when meeting a potential builder for the first time is don't dress like an idiot. Under no circumstances should you wear anything outlandish such as a dress. In a builder's mind, anyone in a dress is an idiot.

Also, say as little as possible. When technological terms and materials are mentioned, nod knowingly, repeating the technical references in each sentence in a meaningful way. It is probable that the term *RSJ* (rolled steel joist) will be used in initial conversations. Builders love to get RSJ into any sentence, especially when talking about knocking through your sitting-room wall. Non-builders know RSJs as big beams made from steel. Get the builder on your side by referring nostalgically to RSJs. Say something like, 'Ah yes, the dear old RSJ. I am looking forward to having more of them in the house.' Any two numbers used together separated by the word *by* indicates he is referring to measurements of timber. Hence, four-by-two, two-by-one, six-by-eight, etc. are all measurements in inches, which tell you the builder has not embraced metric standards. You can intimidate him with your knowledge by going metric. Nod while saying, 'Ah yes, the 1,200 by 600',[15] leaving him to translate. Other

---

[15] These are millimetres. Some people use centimetres, but that seems less scientific to me.

topics will reference insulation, ventilation, concrete slabs and windows. If he mentions earthquake-proofing measures, you will know that you have a cowboy on your hands. If you have some expertise in DIY, chance a reference to Tec-7 such as 'We can use Tec-7 to hold that wall in place and deal with any cosmetic imperfections in the finish.' But in general, if you feel that you must contribute to the conversation or are naturally gregarious, confine all of your comments to your desired finishes such as paints, wallpapers and curtains. Any fool can pick a colour. Don't forget that this is a two-way interview, where the builder will quickly and accurately assess how much about the building game you know. His conclusions will be deduced as much from what you say as how you look.

Don't be surprised when the builder turns up in a green velveteen suit, top hat and a stick-on bright-red beard. It's my uncle, the leprechaun builder, come to assess your vulnerability.

The Credulity Rule

A general rule that comes into play before work begins is that you, the client, should be hugely optimistic, credulous and fully confident that a decent builder will be found, and that the job will go smoothly without delays and general catastrophes. You should also believe that your extension would stay up for years to come. This rule points to an innate characteristic of Irish people in our daily interactions with the world at large: despite our fatalistic outlook, we operate on the principle of hope over experience. Credulity is the beginning of all building work. This impacts the overall experience by producing stress when things inevitably go wrong. It is not unusual to meet people in recovery from a building experience who are threatening to, or have already sought, psychiatric help. They will be heard to say:

'Never again. I could never go through that again. Not for any amount of money.' However, within eighteen months, or less, they start gazing critically at their walls, daydreaming about how they might be improved, where they might be moved to and what new RSJs might be installed. Thus, it starts all over again.

The Misery Rule

While a building project is underway, the whole thing has to be experienced as 'a living hell'. It is mandatory to find the experience 'unbelievably stressful'. Stress is caused by the structural failure on the part of the builder to manage the client's expectations. I say 'structural' because, as we are dealing with engineering, this neglect is built into the process and can be expressed mathematically.

Emulating the great mathematician and physicist Isaac Newton, the misery rule can be expressed axiomatically: the sum of misery experienced over the entire duration (T) of a building project (P) is a constant M. T is variable (normally twice what the builder says it will be) and M is not evenly distributed over T. This means that if the builder thinks his client is not sufficiently miserable, he will exponentially increase the misery quotient towards the end of P to achieve M.

Some people hire architects in the vain hope that the misery can be lessened. This is especially the case on Dublin's Southside. The presence of an architect in the drama does not affect the operation of the misery rule. It simply means that it is a posher project. In fact, the architect will quickly become a source of misery, contributing to M in equal measure with the builder. As one Southside client put it: 'Having an architect just meant I was pissed off with everyone.'

A practical example of the misery rule is the window rule, where waiting for windows is designed to maximise misery.

The window rule is a sub-rule of the broader misery rule. You can think of it as a subplot in a tragic play with audience participation.

The Waiting-for-Windows Rules

Windows can only be ordered from the notorious window supplier – the villain – once the builder has put the *opes*[16] in place. These opes are the actual dimensions for doors and windows, rather than the theoretical ones specified on the project drawings. If there actually are drawings, the proposed dimensions are usually supplied by architects who are the spear carriers in this drama. The difference between the actual and proposed opes is always significant. Since the builder cannot, or will not, say what the actual opes will be before they materialise on site, it is impossible to plan ahead. The builder will account for the difference by blaming the architect, the temperature of the bricks, the colour of the mortar, family stress or anything that immediately comes to mind. Once the actual opes are in place, enter the window-supplier, the most notorious of the subcontractors.

These villains will ultimately be blamed for everything that subsequently goes wrong. Window suppliers have a private language when it comes to estimating times of delivery. This private language is designed to bring a false comfort to the client and avoid sudden trauma. Instead, the suffering is drip-fed over the weeks. They prefer you to quietly fade away while waiting for the windows. Here is a simple conversion table of window-supplier timescales that can lessen the stress: five window-supplier weeks translates to eight normal weeks as you and I would experience them; eight is eleven and twelve is eighteen. If you can remember

---

[16] Opes is slang for openings, which is the term builders use instead of holes, which is what they actually are.

this in advance, you will be fine, but the window supplier will give you his time of delivery with such confidence you will become confused. This confusion will lead to misery.

All work stops until the windows and doors arrive. It is usual to meet dazed neighbours dragging themselves like zombies along the street who, on you enquiring about their renovation, will tell you they are 'waiting on the windows'. When waiting for windows, it is best to spend your time out of your shell of a house on a park bench or hanging around the supermarket aisles. That is where most people in that situation congregate.

The windows will eventually arrive on site and, several weeks later, the specialist subcontractors will install them. There is a contemporary trend of fitting the new windows with the handles on the outside. We live in hard times so many of us can sympathise with doing whatever we can to make life easier for our population of burglars. But there are some spoilsports who insist on the old-fashioned approach of having the handles on the inside. In those cases, the windows have to be taken out, new ones ordered, and the wait begins all over again. This actually happened to me. I ordered a floor-to-ceiling opaque window for our new bathroom. The window that eventually arrived had transparent glass with the handles on the outside. When I pointed out this design feature to the specialist subcontractor, he told me that I could climb up a ladder on the outside to lock the window from there and then I would have 'no problemo'. When I pointed out that I would be on full nude display to the neighbours, he said that he 'wouldn't tell anyone how they should live'. When I asked how long it would take to replace them, he sucked the air in through his teeth, rolled his eyes skyward and came up with a new figure. We returned to waiting for windows. For a while there I was seriously tempted to stick with what had been installed. But this is what they want. They want to wear you down.

The Amnesia Rule

Time heals our wounds. Just weeks after the builders have finally gone, the trauma starts to fade from memory, including the waiting for windows. This is typical of our experience of pain. Women forget the actual pain of childbirth, which facilitates them going through it all again for the sake of the population. Amnesia sets in when we try to recall the specifics of a previous building job. The builder exploits this loss of memory.

For example, on the topic of the proposed timescale for the build, T (above), it is very important but impossible to keep in mind that the length of time for the build proposed by the builder should be at least doubled. Builders halve the actual build time when telling clients how long a job will take. Clients believe them, even when they have hard-won experience. You might ask, 'Are you sure?' just to demonstrate interest or politeness that you are still following the conversation. The builder will reply, 'Sure I'm sure. No problemo.'

Builders like demolishing things, even essential supporting walls and pillars, at the beginning of a project because demolition gives an excellent impression of a good start and causes the client to falsely believe that the builder's T will be accurate. In my own case, the proposed build time was four months, which I foolishly thought was an estimate worked out scientifically by Phil, my builder. It took ten. D'oh!

On-the-Job Rules

So you have dressed for the occasion, you have put aside all of your worries and you have hired a builder. He has under-estimated the build time and over-priced the cost, but you have a steely determination to see it through and be the first person you know to come out on the other side unscathed.

Before your builder turns up at your house for his first very short day, you should be aware of a few general rules to keep in mind when dealing with him in a day-to-day relationship. There are specific rules that govern the behaviour of builders once they are on site. First, there is the desire-to-be-somewhere-else rule that governs the yearning of the builder to be anywhere other than in your house. They will turn up on site only to leave immediately. They will use a myriad of excuses, usually involving sourcing obscure plumbing parts, to get away. Second, there is the positive-future-tense rule, where the builder confines himself to talking only about what will happen on site at some future date, rather than what is actually happening at that moment in time. Third, there is the sharp-intake-of-breath rule, where the builder draws air in through his teeth as a stalling device. This rule allows the builder to develop an excuse to fit the circumstance in the length of time it takes him to start breathing again. Let's see examples of these rules on site.

The Out-of-Site-Is-Better Rule

The contractor will turn up slightly ahead of schedule on the first morning. He will point to his watch, while loudly praising himself for his punctuality. Then he will look both the most impressed and most surprised by his presence, and will ask you to confirm how brilliant he is by saying: 'Look at that. What do you think of that? I said I would be here and here I am.' This will be the last time for months that he will be able to make that utterance. He will immediately propose a celebratory cup of tea to mark the auspicious occasion. He will invade your kitchen with his full crew specially deployed for the morning and start looking around for the most important tool on the job, the kettle. For conversation he may ask where you keep the fig rolls. Everyone will settle down to study the sporting pages of *The Star*.

Once the tea has been drunk, the contractor will stand up to begin the play. He will ask his well-rehearsed sidekick if he brought a particular invaluable tool with him, without which no progress can be made. The contractor will loudly abuse his subordinate for neglecting to bring the specified tool. He will then head off to the building suppliers to 'pick up' some named tool or device, promising to return immediately. That is the last you will see of him for weeks. You will eventually discover that his main function as site manager is to source parts for his workmen. Particularly heavy parts will need to be sourced by the entire crew, who will all disappear together.

Once you get onto the plumbing stage, you will find that, as the plumber inches his way along each pipe, he will be missing a vital component at each bend and junction. When you get past all the junctions back to the automatic valve system for temperature zones, it is best to just go on holidays because you will discover that the very largest heating suppliers tend not to stock any of the relevant parts.

Here is a really good business idea that you would imagine should work but it won't: buy a huge truck and stuff the back of it with every plumbing and electrical device you can find. Park it outside a building site, letting the victims inside know that you are outside and that, if the plumber or sparks need anything, you're on hand. However, the builders would closely examine your merchandise to note what you don't have so that they can return later to ask for one or two of those. They might also ask for imaginary parts that you should try to stock.

On the next morning that you actually see the contractor on site, he will receive a precisely timed phone call on his ever-ringing mobile, which he will purport to be from a client who is in greater need than you. This call may well be from his wife, a crew member hiding behind a partition wall for the occasion or just his phone alarm. There are always clients with greater needs than you. He will tell you that he has to leave to rescue some distressed woman and that he will be back in a *mo, jiff* or *sec*, which you will discover are all considerable lengths of time, sometimes stretching into weeks.

Another technique that builders use to remove themselves from a site is to arrange minor accidents, which oblige them to exit the scene speedily, usually holding a hand under the opposing armpit. On my build, we had two builders in A&E at the same time. One contrived to put his head through a window, while the other slashed his arm with the resulting broken glass. Both were taken away by the contractor in his van (that also functions as a general ambulance), one clutching his head while the other held his injured arm under his armpit. Apparently they were hospitalised for a month. In general, it is important for a builder not to injure himself to the point where he loses consciousness, making it impossible for him to either exit the site by his own volition or partake in a recuperative mug of tea.

I can only imagine where builders actually go when they hastily leave a building site. I imagine them all congregating together like birds in portacabins, well away from their clients, exchanging anecdotes on how efficiently they removed themselves from sites. Wherever they go, they are guided by the principles of getting away as quickly as possible and staying away for as long as possible.

The builder will give you a phone number that you will naively imagine is either his or one at which you can contact him. You will say, 'I rang you thirty-two times yesterday' when you next see him. He will offer you thirty-two reasons why he couldn't answer, which will include: leaving his phone in the van, his phone falling down the toilet at another job, being in A&E with a mate where no phones are allowed, etc. No excuse will include a confession that the number he gave you was not his.

Building Grammar

When conversing with the builders on those rare occasions when you meet them at the back of your house, you must use the appropriate tense or they will become confused. As mentioned, builders speak in the positive future tense. You should respect their optimism. The contractor will point to a hole in the back of your house, while waving his arms above his head to paint an imaginative picture of what it will look like in the mystic future when the job is finished. It is important to practise this syntax so that you can have a meaningful interaction with the builder when he turns up. That way you will avoid wasting the valuable opportunity.

Here is the scene: the builder has removed the doors and windows from the back of your house. With a mug of tea in one hand and a fig roll in the other, you contemplate the opes together.

> Builder: I will source the very best lintels, RSJs and u-value wallboards for those opes. I know a great window company in Azerbaijan that we must use.
> You: The rain is lashing in right now. Can you just cover it with a few sheets of plywood?
> Builder: Other builders would use rubbish. But not me. Only the very best for this job.
> You: A rat came in last night. Little Johnny woke up screaming when he found him in the bed. Can you not just nail boards up while we are waiting for the Azerbaijani windows?
> Builder: There is a new type of plaster on the market that I don't have with me, but it will be perfect for this job when I get it.
> You: I am really worried about the rising crime rate in the neighbourhood. I would like something to separate my family from the elements while they are asleep at night.

You have taken away the garden walls and the back door so I am really worried.

Builder: I have found a new painter who will do a great job. You won't even know the back of your house was ever off.

[You start sobbing. The builder's phone rings.]

Builder [answering his phone]: I'll be right there. Just keep your hand firmly pressed against the artery.

[You get in your car and drive to the builder supply yard for four sheets of plywood, a bag of nails and a tube of Tec-7.]

The Breathing Rule

On confronting the builder on site with any question what-soever, with the exception of 'Would you like a cup of tea?', he will respond by taking a breath and holding it for as long as possible. This allows him to avoid making any rash responses before he has had time to run the question through the computer-like processes of his mind. For example, if you ask, 'Will you be here tomorrow?', he has to mentally examine the permutation of a variety of clients, when he last visited a particular client, how mentally disturbed they might be in the morning compared with you and, impor-tantly, what excuse he can give to avoid turning up. His default setting is to say, 'Yes, I will be here tomorrow' with-out any consideration of the veracity of the statement. When a builder gives you a straightforward positive response, he is usually lying, or *fibbing* (in his parlance), which is just a white lie. He wouldn't believe himself, so why should anyone else?

If you ask how much something costs, you will notice the builder changing colour to purple, because costings take longer to process mentally than simple lies about being somewhere at a specified time. He will exhale and play for more time with the standard observation: 'Oh, that's a bit complicated because a job like that needs special [fill in an obscure specialised expensive component that necessarily is neither on site nor easily or cheaply sourced].' He also has to extract from you what expectations you have in terms of cost. You can practise this exchange by buying a carpet in Marrakech, Morocco. In haggling for a carpet in Morocco, it is customary for the carpet seller to get things going by naming a ludicrously high price. You should respond by coming in as low as possible without laughing. Importantly, you should not offer any sum whatsoever unless you are actually willing to pay that amount if a deal is struck. When haggling on site with a builder about a contingent cost, the carpet-selling model is inversed. In this case you have to suggest the lowest sum you can say with a serious face. The builder will come back with the highest counter-offer he can make, also with a serious face.

A typical scenario is as follows. The builder calls your attention to the fact that the distances between your radiators are now much longer than he had originally guessed from the drawings. Furthermore, the pipes they are making these days – naturally imported from abroad from some place determined to rip us all off – are not as long as they used to be, so he has to buy more of them than he planned. It is now over to you. Just to get the haggle underway, you ask how many extra pipes he needs. He takes a breath, holds it, and, when purple, tells you it is impossible to tell at this stage until he sees what lengths the pipes are in the builder suppliers. You should now offer a figure to keep the momentum going – three, for instance. Three of anything seems reasonable. It is not too many and it doesn't commit you to a cost because you have not yet agreed a price per pipe. It also allows the builder to make a credible increase on the number. He comes back with: 'You definitely need fifteen more pipes.' While knowing nothing about plumbing, you should not cave in at this point. Say something like,

'I don't know. That seems like a lot. Couldn't you stretch them?' Builders can stretch anything when they need to. You should say, 'I think we could get away with six.' It is important to use the phrase 'get away with' because that is something builders understand. After more breaths and a careful study of your general demeanour, he counters with twelve. You should settle on nine.

Now for the tricky part. You have to ask how much each pipe will cost. Turning deep purple from the mental effort, he gasps, 'It is hard to know these days.' He asks, 'What do you think?' You should suggest that such pipes could be purchased for two euro each. He laughs at your naivety and wonders aloud what planet you are living on. He says that pipes he bought just yesterday for a similar job with elastic distances cost him two hundred and thirty euro each. At this point you should counter with your firm commitment to live in the house without any plumbing. Then walk away. As an afterthought, on your way out of any of the many large gaping holes left in your walls by the builders, say that for ten euro per pipe you would consider the luxury of central heating. He will drop his price accordingly. After an hour, you can agree on eighty-three euro per pipe for seven pipes.

* * *

I am left with only one building wish. I wish that when builders are installing Velux windows in inaccessible vaults they would remove the envelope of installation instructions glued to the glass. That envelope of instructions is going to be there on my window until an archaeologist in the future carefully peels it off to preserve it in a museum.

8

Christmas: Who's Doing the Washing-Up?

Christmas is a time when people of all religions come together to worship Jesus Christ.

(Bart Simpson)

The mainstay of anthropology is the documenting of conventional behaviour. There is nothing as conventional as Christmas. An important feature of Christmas is that it is an anthropological opportunity to study Irish families on their best behaviour.

I usually go abroad in December to a country that doesn't practise Christmas rituals. This is becoming more difficult each year as more and more nations and religions join in this globalised Christian festival. When studying rituals, you shouldn't try to make sense of them; you should just go with the flow. For the sake of anthropological research, I gave up my plans to travel to Ak-Turpak, a village in Kyrgyzstan that is the last outpost of the Christmas resistance movement, to host this cultural phenomenon myself. The gods seemed to be on my side because, for full effect, we had a white Christmas. I had no idea what the point of dreaming of a white Christmas meant until I saw the advantages firsthand.

However, despite mobilising my neighbours to shovel snow onto the roads and pile snowdrifts up against the house, our guests still made it through to be with us for Christmas.

* * *

The Rules of an Irish Christmas

Like most of our festivals, including St Patrick's Day, Halloween and the Galway Races, the Irish Christmas is a relatively recent social invention with many of its principal features imported from abroad. In the past, the Irish Christmas was a modest affair. Traditionally, Irish people would only see fruit, chocolate, biscuits and cakes at Christmas. Rich people even got to eat them. Children received toys only on Christmas Day. In its current materialisation, the Irish Christmas lasts at least twelve days, when we stay home from work with enough food to see us through a limited nuclear conflict. The most important Irish Christmas rituals, which are heralded by eleven months of television advertising, include the putting up of trees and cribs, Santa's visit, marathon drinking sessions, buying and exchanging impractical presents, and gathering reluctant family members, seen only once a year, for dinner.

The Irish Christmas may look like Christmas anywhere else. However, there are important differentiating social features under the surface. In Ireland we do Christmas differently. The Irish Christmas Day has the highest incidence of coronary failure of any day of the year; Stephen's Day has the highest incidence of domestic violence; and January sees a peak in post-festivity suicides. Killing a family member or killing yourself are all traditional practices during the Irish Christmas. Very few tourists come to Ireland for Christmas Day to stay with Irish families, which is surprising and must be because they don't realise what they are missing.

If we are relatively laid back for the rest of the year, we make up for it in stress at Christmas. This is sociologically appropriate because the festival of Christmas has its origins in social inversion. We are different at Christmas. Everyone pretends to believe in Santa Claus to get their children to bed early so that we can get pissed in peace on Christmas Eve. We smell good for a few days because we splash on the latest celebrity-sponsored perfumes and aftershave lotions. We model bumper-pack socks for those who gave them to us, just to show that we care, before passing them on to a local charity. We exclaim with hammy delight when unwrapping slippers in the shape of small furry animals, coffee-table books on the television personalities of the Outer Hebrides or the *Complete Guide to Thermal Underwear Patterns of the Antipodes*. I never buy these practical items during the year because I know some thoughtful person will be getting them for me for Christmas. I find it useful to make a list of these potential gifts to send round to my relations so that I won't be disappointed.

If you happen to experience Christmas as the empty kernel at the heart of contemporary consumer society, it is because, in the words of many a world-weary Irish adult, you think, 'Sure, Christmas is only for children.' But that's where you are wrong. Children's Christmas takes up just ten minutes: five minutes on Christmas Eve to wrap the plastic toys (bought while drunk on the way home in the evening from the office Christmas lunch[17]) and stick them under the tree, including putting the tree back upright after knocking

---

[17] The time it takes to actually get home from the office lunch doesn't count, but you might add the eight minutes it takes to get your eyes to focus on the crumpled letter to Santa, plus the one hour and eleven minutes it takes to find the letter in the inside pocket of your jacket that you left on the back of the seat in the pub, which you have to go back for and subsequently stay for just one more.

it over (you will re-attach the decorations in the morning); and another five minutes on Christmas morning to take photographs of the expressions of joyous horror on your children's faces before taking two Solpadeine dissolved in a brandy and ginger ale. The rest of the time is for the adults.

Unlike the origins of many rituals, we know relatively a lot about the genesis of Christmas. The festival originates from the Roman Saturnalia.[18] The great festival of Saturn was celebrated on the nineteenth of December. The Emperor Caligula, who must have been of Irish stock, had the good sense to add an extra day to the celebrations, which he dedicated to the sport of the young, called *dies juvenalis*, which may have taken the form of sports competitions between children and lions. During the festival of Saturnalia, the slave became the master of the house for a day. This social inversion brought about the chaos of the celebrations that reinforced the merits of the old order in the minds of the participants, including the slaves, when it was all over. The modern-day equivalent of this chaos in the Irish household on Christmas Day is the panic about cooking dinner or running out of vital essentials such as wrapping paper, mince pies, cake decorations, crackers, chocolates, mixers for drinks and cocktail sticks. People become panicked about their relatives coming to visit. Family members gather from all around in order to help drive each other mad. As in Rome, the old order of things is embraced with renewed zeal after the festival has ended and everyone has left. Collapsing immediately after the visitors have gone, we ritually exclaim: 'Thank God that's over for another year!' We then rush back to work in mid-January with a renewed apprecia-

---

[18] Saturnalia coincides with the mid-winter solstice festival marking the shortest day of the year. Some historians trace the origins of Christmas to this but anthropologists know that Christmas Day is actually the longest day of the year.

tion of our old routines. By late September, we start asking each other what we are doing for Christmas. We have a choice between two options: we are either staying put with people coming to us or we are the ones doing the visiting. Both options cause panic.

The Rules of Putting Up the Tree

Another important Christmas ritual is the putting up of the Christmas tree. Like most rituals, it makes no sense. The first formal step is to discuss the putting up of the tree with your neighbours as a topic of ritualistic conversation. Your annual conversation about the Christmas tree should typically go as follows:

You: Have you put up your tree?

Neighbour: Not yet. Plenty time for that. What about yourself?

You: I think I will go for a fake one this year. I am sick of the pine needles getting all over the carpet; the dog kept pissing against the trunk. After the fire last year I am seriously thinking of going fake.

Neighbour: I hear Woodies have a very convincing imitation tree.

You: I was there yesterday and they only have the white ones left.

Neighbour: Oh God, no. You couldn't go with a white one. They're so tacky.

You: I'll wait until next weekend to see what they have down at Matt's.

Neighbour: You're probably right. Let me know how you get on.

The following week you meet again:

You: Do you know where I can get my hands on a tree? Matt has none. He says he can't get anything this year. He had only a few two-foot-high things and they went out the door within an hour. I have looked the length and breadth of the city but can't find anything except a massive thing for three hundred euro that I couldn't get into the house without taking the ceiling down. I don't mind for myself but the kids will be very disappointed if I can't find a tree. It's really only for the children.

Neighbour: I couldn't find anything either. Apparently there is some disease that has wiped out whatever kind of tree they use for Christmas. I got the last white one up in Woodies. When I was at the till someone tried to buy it from me for eighty quid. There was no box with it so I only paid twenty-five. My kids are getting big now so they don't care what colour it is. I was actually surprised. It looks okay. If you squint at it after a few pints when the fairy lights are on it looks like it's covered in snow.

You: What am I going to do for a tree? I wonder if there is any kind of a bush in the garden I could get away with? What am I going to do?

Twenty-Four hours later:

You: I am going out of my mind looking for a tree. As if I haven't enough to do already!

Neighbour: Maggie said she would leave me if the white one stays so I am still on the hunt for a tree. I heard there were Chinese trees for sale up in Glasnevin. I am going up there now.

You: What's a Chinese tree?

Neighbour [sighing]: A tree sold by people from China!

A week later – five days after Christmas:

Neighbour: How did you get on with the tree?
You: Ah, I didn't bother this year. I think they are all a bit vulgar, really. Mind you, you would miss them. The dog missed having a tree. The children didn't care. They had their toys. It's not the same really without a tree. How did you get on?
Neighbour: I brought the white one back in from the bin after Maggie stormed off to her mother's for the dinner. It did the job fine. I must remember to be more organised next year. Are you all set for Paddy's Day in March?
You: Yes, but I still have a few things to do.

Bad Santa

Christmas is a time for giving. Where there is giving, there is taking. The custom of giving gifts to children was originally part of the pagan festival of Saturnalia, but it eventually became associated with the Three Wise Men when Christmas became a Christian festival. When Santa Claus started bringing us gifts, it became a pagan festival again.

We think of Santa Claus as a genial harmless old man, but he is really a bit of a queer fish. His past is very dodgy. Some historians believe that he evolved from Odin, the Yule-Father, who rides across the sky on a horse, carelessly dropping gifts onto sleeping children. Others believe he comes from Melchior, who is one of the Three Wise Men. Most commonly, it is thought that he is actually St Nicholas, the patron saint of children, virgins of marriageable age, sailors, merchants, travellers, prostitutes, pawnbrokers, choirboys, thieves and hardened general sinners. He is also found in the company of transsexual Norse goddesses, fairies, gnomes, witches, drag acts from Russia, virgins, as well as necrophiles and cannibals. Because Santa is not part of traditional Irish folklore, we know little about him. He is in fact a blow-in. When we examine his reputation abroad, it is obvious that he is very suspect. But no one here seems to mind.

Before coming to Ireland, Santa travelled around the world, changing both his appearance and behaviour along the way. Historically speaking, St Nicholas travelled from Southern Italy to Britain. On the way, he passed through Russia, where he acquired his white beard, his sledge, Rudolph and the rest of the reindeer. From Russian folklore we get the practical advice not to walk under these reindeer as they fly across the sky at night. From Russia, Santa made his way to Germany and Holland. In seventeenth-century Holland, Santa, aka St Nicholas, only visited good children, while his sinister cousin, Black Peter, took bad children, or Catholics as they were also called at that time, to Spain. After some years in the New World, Santa, abandoning his sledge for a liner, crossed the Atlantic to Victorian Britain. From there, it was a short ferry trip to Rosslare in Ireland.

When I was a child, I used to leave Guinness and Christmas cake out for Santa. Nowadays, because Irish children are more health conscious, they leave non-alcoholic drinks and carrots for both Rudolph and Santa. We didn't have a thought for Rudolph when I was young. Santa's high-blood-pressure complexion convinced me that he preferred the booze. His fondness for chimneys brings him into disrepute because of their folk association with nasty supernatural characters such as witches and goblins. His connection with roofs, where he parks his sleigh before squeezing his bulk down the chimneys, is equally damaging for his reputation in that it links him with the hormone-treated Norse goddess Freya, who drove her chariot, drawn by cats, across roof-tops while sporting a beard. Traditionally, roofs and chimneys are the exclusive territory of female supernatural beings. Santa's weakness for these hints at a sexual ambiguity in his nature. Is there something he needs to tell us? Is there something he needs to tell himself?

St Nicholas is venerated as the patron saint of children, especially little boys, because of his legendary restoration to life of three boys who had been killed and dismembered by a wicked innkeeper who preserved their parts in brine to serve to his hungry customers for dinner. He supposedly gets the red of his suit from the sleeves getting soaked in the boys' blood. Santa is found at crime scenes all over Europe. Where there is death and mayhem, Santa is sure to be near at hand. For instance, in Italy there were three young unmarried sisters, the daughters of an impoverished nobleman, who had no dowries. Their father decided to turn them to prostitution, but to 'save' them Santa visited each of them on three consecutive nights. He gave each a bag of gold. In most circumstances, being caught giving money to prostitutes means only one thing. But Santa's plea of 'Just trying to help, your honour' actually worked to keep his incredibly nice-guy reputation intact. Interestingly, this is the character we allow to sneak into our children's rooms at night to give them presents. This is the guy we use to threaten our children if they misbehave. Confusing or what?

But Santa seemed to have cleaned up his act when he was taken on by Coca-Cola. Thanks to a corporate makeover, Santa Claus has become the Teflon old geezer with no criminal record. In this age of registering sex offenders, he has charmed his way into all our homes. However, my suspicions remain.

The Rules of Give and Take

So you had better watch out, you'd better not shout, Santa Claus is coming to town. Is it any wonder, with Santa Claus at the helm of gift-giving, that giving and receiving gifts at

Christmas is fraught with difficulty? The rules for giving gifts involve knowing what to get for each type of recipient. The rules of getting gifts involve knowing what to expect from whom. Don't panic. It is all very conventional.

As Christmas fast approaches, both the stress and feelings of guilt increase exponentially. Secular Ireland has replaced religion with gift-giving because it has the same effect of making us feel bad about ourselves. If you are rich, you can hire someone to do your present-buying for you. If not, you can beg someone to do it. As it is difficult to find someone who is not already begging someone else, you will probably end up doing your own shopping. Put it off for as long as possible. Then run around the shops on Christmas Eve with an hour to go before closing. The results will be the same as if you bought your presents in the previous spring sales.

It is easier to shop for Christmas presents for Irish women because they are open to a wider range of acceptable options. Golf was invented specifically to allow Irish males to buy other Irish males presents without attracting any embarrassing suspicion about the motivation involved. An Irish male can buy anyone a box of golf balls or a putter. If stuck, you can buy golf balls for your entire family and friends. If they don't play golf, you can suggest they should take it up for the New Year. Golf balls are also useful ballast to bulk up a lightweight present such as a pair of socks. You should not give toiletries to anyone who has a well-established body odour. BO remains one of the most intractable social problems in Ireland. It is a mainstay of our personal-help columns. Only give soap to the well-washed to avoid trouble. Clothes also present challenges because you may get the sizes wrong. Always err on the side of the size being too large because you can say, 'Oh, I see you have lost a lot of weight since we last met', rather than 'Oh, I didn't realise you were so fat.' Before handing the garment over, tell the recipient that you are willing to change it. But remember, only the very confident or the completely desperate buy their relatives clothes for Christmas.

Irony Rules, Okay?

Happily, most Irish families have members living overseas. As Christmas is the time when we are driven by an innate impulse to congregate, many distant members fly in just to be with their loved ones. The general rule at Irish family gatherings is that you should only discuss topics in which you have no real interest. If you marry into an Irish family and find yourself under pressure to come to Ireland for Christmas to be with your new in-laws, you will find this rule practically life saving. As a stranger, your novel presence will bring about an artificial improvement in behaviour that will last about fifty-six minutes. After that, everyone will revert to their normal selves, having exhausted their entire supply of fake manners. The rule of avoiding meaningful themes is designed to delay conflict and allow for full deniability when the inevitable conflict does erupt. You don't want to be 'the one who started it'.

There is a conversation rule, which is well understood in the context of particular family histories. In general, start with indifference and move on to irony. The older and more senior the family members, the more ironic their comments should eventually become as the day goes on and the sherry intake increases. Do not ask a direct question unless, like a lawyer, you already know the answer. If you ask a direct question, someone may give you a direct answer, which will trigger the rule of crying and rushing from the room. The traditional way to ironically indicate total disagreement with a point of view when you are a visiting relation at Christmas is to start your remark with the Hiberno-English phrase 'I suppose', which means in English that you don't suppose at all.

When you tire of drivelling on non-consequential topics or when your confidence grows, you can move onto ironic comments. In this case, the conversation game is to appear be as sincere as possible about views that are the opposite of those you actually hold. Evasion and irony should take you through your entire visit if you concentrate and keep off the booze. There is a rule that if you do have a lapse in concentration caused by your twenty-seventh glass of wine, the other participants in the conversation are allowed to remind you of your indiscretion for fifteen future Christmases.

While you may be burning to ask a direct question, you should translate it first into an indifferent query and then into irony. Following traditional Irish familial conversation custom, you should not ask your uncle if his new wife is worried that what happened to his previous wife may happen to her. Rather, enquire how he thinks Cork will do next year in the hurling. Both weather and sport were invented to allow Irish family members to converse at great length with each other without saying anything dangerous. You should put some effort into your Hiberno-English translations to demonstrate your commitment to domestic harmony. You can translate the sentence 'I suppose your new missus won't go down the stairs ahead of you' into 'I suppose your wife is very happy with the new stair rails!' 'I suppose you're sure you are the father of that child?' can be transformed to 'I suppose a lot of black-haired fathers have blonde children.'

For example, one mother-in-law casually remarked when presented with her daughter-in-law's Christmas cooking: 'I suppose I am very broadminded. I am happy to try anything.' When you open a particularly disappointing present, you should say, 'I suppose I will find a use for that', or 'I suppose I'm grateful to get anything at all', or 'I suppose I can wear that in public.' When you are eventually encouraged to leave for your own house at 1.00 a.m.

on St Stephen's morning by your exhausted hosts who are standing beside you with your coat and hat, you can say, 'I suppose I could call a taxi', just before starting into another beer and recycled turkey sandwich.

From a standpoint outside of the Irish family, it is easy to confuse complaining with unhappiness. But, for us, complaining is just a habit we have gotten into. We are never happier than when we are having a good moan about each other. Couples who have been happily married for years routinely express their devotion by complaining about each other to anyone who cannot get away. This is because, being Irish, we are too embarrassed and definitely too emotionally inhibited to use affectionate language in public. Married couples are often so obsessively in love with each other that they complain all day long, every day. After Christmas, devoted wives will get together in golf clubs or at coffee mornings to compete with each other over which husband deserves the accolade for being the most neglectful, most thoughtless and most useless around the house.

What Applies to *Them* and *Us*

Divide your kinship system into *them* and *us*. Those who normally live in your house on all the other days of the year are *us*; all those others in your house on Christmas Day are *them*. You can alleviate the stress of having Christmas guests by drinking straight vodka from coffee mugs. Even if you have an established alcohol problem, it is best not to call attention to it by drinking straight from the bottle on Christmas Day. Pour a large measure of vodka into a number of festive mugs and leave them strategically around the house for *us*. This way, you and your family can give the impression that you are just enjoying a sociable coffee together. If you like, ask *them* to join you in a coffee, but remember to serve them coffee and not vodka; coffee, not vodka. When you eventually fall over on the floor laughing or crying, or both, or you sag into a corner and snore, the more sober members of your vodka-in-coffee-cup drinking circle can excuse your behaviour by telling the rest of your guests that you are just exhausted from all the work you put in to make this Christmas special for *them*.

Christmas Dinner Conversation Rules

Corral your guests together, herding them with a ladle, and ply them with drinks. This will both improve their appetites and dull their critical faculties. Don't serve a starter for Christmas dinner because it is too difficult to manage a main course, dessert and secret drinking on top of a starter. If desperate to make an impression, allow them to suck on half a grapefruit, which you prepared earlier by halving it.

There is a significant literature on how to produce a moist turkey, but what it ignores is the fact that most Irish people, while they won't admit to it, secretly like dry turkey. One informant told me that, coming up to Christmas, he worries that his wife will discover a technique that actually works for producing a moist turkey. Once the turkey has been placed in the oven, it should be henceforth referred to as *the bird*, that is not your brother's new girlfriend. As the fear of turkey-based food poisoning is a deeply embedded national food anxiety, turkeys should roast in the oven for twenty minutes per pound of meat plus eight hours. If you actually over-do it, you can use a saline drip to revive the turkey.

Remove the bird from the oven, allowing it to rest while the male members of the family compete to carve. This should take about thirty minutes. If you hope to win the right to carve, you should be otherwise unfamiliar with a kitchen or be unable to use a knife. But you should be able to subdue the competing males using drunken headlocks and menacing behaviour with an electric carving knife. Don't threaten to sulk for the rest of the day if you are unsuccessful, because then you will only be playing into your host's hands.

Once the bird is hacked and served, the cook should open the dinner conversation by asking the diners to comment on the relative moisture content of the turkey. Diners will also be asked to draw comparisons with previous Christmas turkeys. It is customary for the cook to ask, 'What do you think of the bird? Do you think it is too dry?' This is a ritual, so remember, without reference to the reality on your plate, the customary response is 'No, it is very nice. Very moist. Delicious. Hmnnn. Hmnnnn. Can I have more gravy please?' After this ritualistic response, you will be invited to compare it with last year's turkey, regardless of the fact that you were in Aksai Chin last year avoiding Christmas. You should affect an exact memory of last year's bird, responding with 'This year's bird is much better.' At this point, inquire about the unique cooking technique, which allows you to pretend that you actually have some interest in the state of the bird. Your host will take you through Richard Corrigan's recommendations, which they followed, but adding their own twist.

While you will not be asked to comment on the quality of the vegetables in the same detail, you may be asked to remark positively on the variety and whether or not the carrots are cooked to your liking. Before you can respond, you will be told that we Irish have an unfortunate habit of over-cooking our vegetables and that it is really for your own self-improvement as a gourmand that you are being exposed to *al dente* carrots. This is because your host should have forgotten to cook the carrots because they were in a pot under the kitchen table, which, following annual custom, were discovered only a minute before dinner was served.

Ever more varieties of vegetables have been added to the traditional Irish Christmas dinner menu. No contemporary traditional dinner is complete without fifteen varieties of vegetable, including arracacha and nopales. You should serve bread sauce, onion sauce and gravy – and tomato ketchup because you will have forgotten the cranberry sauce. On Christmas morning, observe the ritual of calling on your neighbour to borrow cranberry sauce, which they should also have forgotten to buy. Stay for a gin and tonic that you are allowed to drink from a glass. You should demonstrate at least five potato-cooking techniques – because you are Irish – including baked, roast, boiled, gratin and one of your own devising.

Polite Irish Christmas dinner conversation typically takes the form of monologues that can run in parallel – but we don't like to talk about ourselves. Popular soliloquies include relating in minute detail the opinions and attitudes of strangers that you met on a train or plane; people you met in your psychiatrist's waiting room; or people you read about in the newspaper. If you run out of factual information, because the subject of your monologues is unknown to everyone else, you can endlessly improvise by adding illuminative detail at will. Before you start, be as confident as possible that no one present knows those you choose to monologue about. Remember, in polite Irish conversation an evergreen subject is to relate the successes of the children of complete strangers to your own children. Christmas dinner is the best time for Irish parents to report on how their children's old classmates are doing. Irish Christmas dinner conversation between mothers and daughters should take the form of a monologue as follows:

Mother: When I met B [insert the name of any unknown person frequently referenced on family occasions] last week, she told me that her eldest, M – you remember M? She was in school with you. No? That is funny. I was sure you would remember her. She won the school millennium prize for her outstanding contributions to scholarship, sport and international charity fundraising in her final year. She was in all the papers. She was on the telly. Surely you remember her? No? How strange. You remember she was tall with that beautiful hair and skin. Not a spot. Not a blemish. She never missed a day out of school. You were probably in hospital having your acne operation on the day of the award ceremony. Well, never mind, but you should get that memory checked out. I believe drink is very bad for the memory cells in your brain. Anyway, where was I? Oh yes. B was telling me that after M qualified as a paediatrician, she saved the lives of literally millions of babies in Africa. She is now married to the president of a pharmaceutical company that provides reduced-price condoms to HIV victims in the Third World. When she was young she kept her head down and concentrated on her studies, waiting for the right man to come along. She didn't allow herself to become pregnant at sixteen and end up with someone who doesn't even know what a condom is. She has two beautiful children, one of each – a boy and girl. Neither of them is stunted with a learning disorder because she didn't smoke or drink when she was pregnant. They live in a wonderful house overlooking the sea. Her mother tells me that she is the happiest person in Ireland. *I suppose* we are all happy in our own way.

The particular daughter to whom the monologue is addressed should throw down her cutlery, scream that she 'can't stand this anymore', and rush from the room. Her sisters should say that they will bring her back. The daughter should have fled to a room where festive mugs of gin have been pre-hidden for this eventuality. The sisters should drink the gin and exchange small talk about how well they think the day is going before returning to dinner.

Someone will say, 'For God's sake, Mother. Can you talk about something else? J went to a lot of trouble cooking dinner for you.' Mother will say, 'What have I said? I was just telling you how well M is getting on. I thought you would have been happy for her. I suppose I will say nothing at all. Just keep my mouth shut. Saying nothing is the best policy. Poor Mrs R was telling me last week about how she is confined to bed after her gall-bladder operation went badly wrong when the doctors removed her spleen by accident...'

If, between courses, you ask your sister-in-law how her attempts to have a baby are going, you know that you are drunk. Switch to water for forty minutes.

Then there is the silent relative who rarely speaks except to grunt to confirm that they are still alive. These are to be cherished and should be a chair-filler at all your family events.

Rules for Having Arguments

In general, the volume of continuous complaining accompanying each dinner course is an indication of how well a Christmas dinner is going. While you have done your best up to this point to deflect or postpone conflict, once seated at the dinner table it is important to get the family quarrels underway as quickly as possible. Don't leave people waiting. Once everyone is seated, it is polite to kick-off immediately. Irish people cause family arguments in order to get attention – any form of attention is better than being ignored. As Oscar Wilde used to say when he still lived in Ireland, 'There is only one thing worse than fighting with your family, and that's not fighting with them.'

After dinner you can compete walrus-like for some space on the couch, where you then lie, stunned, watching *Willy Wonka and the Chocolate Factory*. If you are feeling more agile, you can play a board game or a game of cards. Or you can participate in a family row.

The rules of family rows are straightforward. One participant gets the row going and at least one other keeps it going.

Some of my relations have been known to take on both roles simultaneously, so if you are on your own for Christmas you can play the solitaire version. Family-based arguments and resentments require the participants to have extraordinary memories which continue to function under the influence of alcohol. Take any one of three common approaches to get the argument underway. First, there is the *who has always been treated better than whom and by whom* discussion. This is where one family member voices the view that another member of the family, preferably a sibling, has historically been routinely treated better by a parent than them and/ or anyone else. The examples offered of unequal treatment should relate back to incidents that happened at least twenty years ago. This family row scenario should ideally refer-ence frequently rehearsed incidences involving larger dolls, better clothes, being allowed to stay out longer or more often when young, being taken on more holidays, getting more pocket money and getting better presents at Christ-mas. If the participants are very drunk, a parent should be accused of *loving* the other sibling more. This will cause a very sudden embarrassed silence that will allow for glasses to be re-filled. You should also make time for the other participants to remember their grievances. But use the *love* word extremely sparingly and only if the row is in danger of fizzling out. A variation on this theme is to repeat the view that, while everyone was treated badly, you were treated worst of all.

The second common approach to starting the family row is to speculate aloud who amongst the participants is most likely to be the beneficiary of the single, elderly, ill and very rich potential benefactress aunt, who is at this time passed out in the corner of the couch. This is the *who is getting the old bag's money* discussion. The opening gambit can lead to the more interesting version of this row, focussing on who deserves to be left everything. Each candidate should list their reasons why they should be the one, illustrating their argument with examples of good deeds that they did for their aunt. There is no need to wait for another player to finish their reasons before shouting out yours. Satisfactory examples of behaviour meriting inheritance include visiting every other year, not returning phone calls to avoid rows, begging money off her for your round-the-world trip, stealing cigarettes from her handbag to help her avoid lung cancer, stealing her handbag and borrowing her car for two years as a road safety measure. Whatever it is you do to show your special affection, don't move the old bat in with you for forty years and 'wait on her hand and foot', because if you do that she will definitely leave you nothing.

The third standard technique for starting a family argument is to ask *whose turn it is to [insert an unpopular familial responsibility, such as hosting Christmas next year or taking your unconscious aunt to the hospital]?*

The older you are the better scope you have for rowing, because you probably only have long-term memory. This means you can draw exclusively on memories from ancient family history, giving you an advantage over younger branches of the family tree. Older relatives can engage in subsidiary rows involving discussions going back over fifty years.

The Irish like to row, so if your newly adopted Irish parents-in-law end up in a headlock, you should say, 'I suppose it's great to see them still so close after so many years together.'

* * *

No account of Christmas is complete without a traditional Christmas recipe. Here is mine, which was handed down to me from my grandfather: the turkey sandwich. The size of the turkey should be at least twice that required to feed everyone at dinner. This allows for the first round of turkey recycling in the form of the turkey sandwich. Avoid goose because it doesn't provide leftover turkey to make sandwiches.

Ingredients: White bread (pre-sliced), butter (lots) – left to sit at room temperature for five hours – mayonnaise (a large blob), cranberry sauce (break into a shop for this because it is essential), cold bread and sausage stuffing, white turkey meat and two layers of turkey skin (crispy, with the sub-dermal fat still on).

Preparation: From start to finish, this recipe takes three hours. Immediately after dinner say you will undertake one of the most important rituals of the Irish Christmas: the washing-up. Make sure you volunteer first before any other dinner guest. Coincidentally, the washing-up will take three hours, even with a dishwasher, because the cook will have used all the utensils, bowls and pots in the kitchen to cook dinner. There are two advantages to doing the washing-up. First, you avoid the after-dinner family discussions. Second, you can source the best ingredients to assemble your turkey sandwich. Spend three hours in the kitchen doing this.

Cooking: Assemble all of the ingredients in layers with the bread on the outside. Consume on your own in the kitchen with a cold bottle of beer. Delicious!

9

Politics: She Doesn't Have the Hair for High Office

Those are my principles. If you don't like them I have others.

(Groucho Marx)

Anthropologists like to investigate political culture from the bottom up. This is what we call producing a subaltern narrative. I thought that it might be interesting to do a top-down study by examining the rules of how to become an Irish politician. What better way to be Irish than to either become a TD or, if you can't achieve that, to vote in an Irish election? I decided that the best way to research the rules on how to get into public office or vote would be to be a fly on the wall during an election campaign. For that I needed two things: I needed an election campaign; and I also needed a candidate who knew the rules and who was going to be elected. The previous Fianna Fáil-led Government has been much criticised but I have no complaints. Almost to the day of my decision to research politics, the Government obligingly collapsed, announcing an election before I could even make my request for one in the interest of social science. The second thing I needed was a good election prospect who would tolerate me stalking him or her.

I knew my neighbour, Pablo Cruise,[19] would be canvassing to become a TD. Pablo gets most of his funding from his mother. He is often slagged off on Twitter for actually bringing his mother canvassing with him. In 2003 he spent forty-eight evenings in a row canvassing door-to-door with his wife and mother when he was a totally unknown aspiring politician. For this election he had a much increased support team, which I was hoping would include me because I decided, in traditional anthropological fashion, to follow him around to find out firsthand what the rules for becoming elected are. This was going to be exciting – I was going to be there from the start to the victorious end on the night of the count.

With my stalking methodology worked out, I set out to put my plans to him. I found him sliding down a hill on a sleigh fashioned from the poster of one of his political rivals. He pointed out that this was a Green Party candidate who should have no objection to his election materials being recycled. He told me to give it a go. I slid down the hill. It is not just politically satisfying to grind the face of your opponent into the dirt (or snow), it is also great fun. To avoid this happening to him during the next snowstorm, Pablo decided to make his posters too small to serve as improvised toboggans. When we had worn out the Green candidate's posters, I put my plan to him. He told me that the party would be

---

[19] Pablo Cruise is not his real name. I am following the long-standing anthropological practice of changing the names of informants. This is sometimes done to preserve anonymity, sometimes for security and sometimes just out of habit. My candidate is our neighbourhood authority on alt-rock, indie rock and contemporary country music, so I thought it fitting to use the name of an obscure eighties band.

nervous about someone following him but that I could go undercover as part of his campaign. I agreed because here was an opportunity to carry out classic participatory research, what the great father of modern social anthropology, Malinowski, called 'participant observation'. Pablo was now officially *my candidate*. Lucky him!

For this research, I knocked on hundreds of doors all over the city centre, attended hustings, rallies and radio programmes, drove cars, bought lunches, debated, argued, wore badges and covered myself in party stickers, drew lines on maps, offered advice, and actually became a supporter of my candidate. In the tradition of anthropological science, I went native.

* * *

Irish political campaigns are not about espousing grandiose ideological theories or testing your assumptions in the arena of informed debate. They are about shouting at other candidates on the telly and knocking on every door in the constituency. My constituency is Dublin Central,[20] which elects four representatives to the Dáil. It has about 65,000 voters living behind 34,000 doors, all of which, ideally, should be knocked on at least once in a month of campaigning. My candidate represents a conservative, some would say right-wing, party, in a predominantly left-of-centre working-class area. The constituency is a mix of ordinary Dubs, elderly Dubs, students who are left-wing until they make enough money to migrate south of the Liffey, migrants from the Southside who couldn't afford Southside housing during the Celtic Tiger boom, and emigrants from

[20] To preserve Pablo's identity, perhaps I should say that maybe it's not Dublin Central.

Africa, Asia and Eastern Europe.[21] There are also a few posh enclaves in the east of the constituency.

I turned up on the first night for training and orientation as a campaigner. I was told that topics that worried voters included employment, the Budget, public sector reform, health and general political reform. For homework I was to study the party position on these topics before meeting the public. The party had usefully set these out in an idiot's guide called the *Five Point Plan*.[22] Over the coming weeks many voters would ask me to remind them 'How many points are there in the Five Point Plan?' If I was having a good day, I would say 'Six!' I also learned that people who don't agree with the party's point of view, generically called Fianna Fáilers, argue with you and people who do agree don't and are usually polite. Supporters of another party will detain you in argument at their door so that you will effectively meet fewer potential voters during the campaign. If you are not getting abused, you are getting interrogated. My job was simple: as one of a pack of campaigners, I would knock on constituency doors asking for votes for my candidate. If they seemed interested or sympathetic, I would ask Pablo, waiting on the footpath out of harm's way, to say hello and shake their hand. I would move on if they were hostile or Fianna Fáilers. If Pablo – who, being political, likes to talk – stayed too long at any door, I would drag him away to the next one. If houses had no front gardens and the doors opened onto the street, it was easy for our pack to relay down an entire terrace with impressive efficiency. If houses had front gardens, someone, i.e. me, had to open and close all the gates so progress was slower. With five or six people in a pack accompanying Pablo, we could relay past each other in a highly organised system.

---

[21] Or maybe it's not. Am I taking this too far?
[22] This anonymity tactic isn't working, is it?

How to Be a Candidate

On my first night of actual campaigning we went to Stoneybatter, where there were no front gardens. I excitedly knocked at my very first door. As the door opened, I opened my mouth to speak the lines I had practised in the mirror that morning but the Stoneybatter woman got in ahead of me with, 'I'm not taking anything off fucking Fianna Fáil,' and immediately slammed the door in my face. I resolved to be faster with my lines. At the next door I blurted out as fast as I could that I was looking for a number one vote for Pablo Cruise. Then I saw that this Stoneybatter man was holding a joint. He was incapable of any sudden movements or decisions. Relaxing, I went on to tell him that I was sorry to disturb his evening but I was campaigning for the upcoming election and... 'I'm not interested,' he told me calmly. 'I'm not interested in anything, man.' And he closed the door.

A few doors later, I got to say my lines again. This time I was told 'You are all a crowd of shaggers.' For the sake of my research, I asked if that was a good thing or a bad thing. The door was slammed so I moved on without clarity. So far I hadn't been able to safely introduce Pablo to anyone.

I got to another door where I had a very animated reception from an elderly couple. From the old man I learned that the collective noun for politicians is a 'shower'. I also learned that when politicians form showers, the most effective way to interact with them is to shoot them. I was told 'You need shooting. My only problem is that I can't decide whether to use a shotgun or a pistol.'

'Now love, don't upset yourself. They're not worth it,' his wife said, patting his arm.

He pushed her inside. 'I'll have my say. I wrote to you shower about the dogs shitting and pissing against that pole,' he said, pointing to a telephone pole on the footpath just outside his house. 'When I got up the other morning there was the shit and piss back again. Yous are all useless. You're all the fucking same.' When Pablo heard the shouting, he came to my rescue. He assured the old man that the situation would be looked into. His wife, who had been nervously standing inside the door, came out and gently led her muttering husband back inside.

At the next door a woman told me that she didn't know what way she was going to vote, but that she was not going to tell me. Fair enough! At another door I found out that because it was a Sinn Féin house it was nothing personal but they had no interest in my policies. At another door I got my first sympathetic reception so I knocked at the next door feeling good. From inside, a voter shouted through the letterbox, 'You have a fucking cheek even knocking on that door whoever the fuck you are. Fuck off the whole fucking lot of you.' I did.

On I went into the dark night. A blue door opened.

'Good evening, Mrs. How are you?'

'I'm fine, pet, if I don't think about it.' The blue door closed.

A brown door opened.

'Fucking shower of bastards.'

'I'm not with Fianna Fáil,' I shouted.

'Oh. Okay so. Sorry.' The brown door closed.

A yellow door opened.

'I'm voting for E.'

'But he isn't a candidate in this constituency,' I calmly pointed out.

'I like him. I'm voting for him anyway so fuck off.' The yellow door closed.

A grey door opened.

'Can you get me a CCTV camera on that fence over there?'

'I'll see what I can do. Can I tell you about our Five Point Plan?'

'I want it pointing down that alley over there because it fills with gurriers every weekend.' The grey door closed.

I knocked on a door with four statues of the Blessed Virgin lined up in the fanlight.

'What's your position on abortion?'

I was taken off guard because my briefing notes didn't cover that. 'Oh no. Not this again. Is it okay if I don't have one?' I respond meekly.

'Abortion is very important to me. I am a seventy-year-old woman who cares about abortion. The EU is gone mad on abortion. How can I vote for you if you won't tell me what your position on abortion is? Come back. Stop running away.'

Another blue door opened.

'Where's Pablo's mother? I want to talk with her.'

'She's not here tonight.'

'She's a lovely woman. Tell her to call round to see me.'

'I will.'

'Good night.'

'Good night,' I said, surprised because I realised that was the first time someone said it to me all evening. The blue door closed.

The next night that I was out canvassing, we had a volunteer from Kansas with us called Daniel. Daniel had contacted the campaign manager through his Facebook account to volunteer for our leaflet drop. After a speedy orientation on the Five Point Plan, he came with me to Cabra.

I was standing a few feet away when Daniel knocked at his very first door, which instantly swung open to reveal a wizened old woman with her fist held above her head ready to strike like a cobra.

'Feck off ye Fianna Fáil bollix!' she shouted at him before he could move his lips. Daniel was conscientious so he wasn't going to be deflected from his mission easily. He thrust out his hand to shake hers and immediately started into his prepared drawl. 'Good evening, ma'am. My name is Daniel. I'm from Kansas. I'm looking for your vote in the election.' She slowly lowered her fist, silently taking a flyer from him while staring with her mouth open in confusion. When we met on the street at the garden gates, Daniel primly remarked that you would never find a sweet little old lady like her calling you a bollix in Kansas.

From door to door the serious issues such as public sector pay, minimum wage, mortgage relief and childcare support came up. But then there were the more pressing issues. One of my fellow campaigners asked a voter when she opened her door:

'Listen missus, we have been out here for hours. Do you mind if I use your loo?'

'I do mind because I don't support you shower.'

'I only want to use your toilet. I'm not asking you to vote for us.'

'What if anyone sees you? They'll think I've gone over to the other side.'

'No one will see me.'

Eventually all eight of us used her toilet.

A black door opened.

'Mister, have you any kids? You can't have because if you had you'd know that you couldn't afford them. I have three but I can't afford even one and you can't send them back. Will your party take two of my kids off of me? Here, take them. Yous can have these two. They're in playschool now. They're more expensive than this one here who is still only a babby. None of you shower will take any of them off me but you won't give me enough money to hold on to them. Here, come back; I have a suitcase packed for the two of them. Come back. I'll only be a minute. Fecking shower! Yous are all useless.'

The black door closed as I ran down the path without the children.

Another night, just before midnight, Pablo picked me up on a street corner to drive me to a national radio station where he was participating in a late night debate. In order to get into the studio, I had to pretend to be his bodyguard. I imagined that those in security who saw me were hoping he wouldn't experience any real threat. He said, 'I hope you're taking note of the rock 'n roll lifestyle of the Irish politician.' I told him I would take note. I sat in the empty dark hall to wait for him while he was in the studio. A few hours later, on the way home in his car, he asked me if I was going to vote for him. I told him that I hadn't yet made up my mind what way I was going to vote. I promised him I would give it serious consideration.

Back on the campaign trail, I learned that the social class of your audience can be determined by the political topics that engage the people you meet at doors. In middle-class homes there are philosophical concerns. For example, a very polite woman told me that she was a humanist. As such, she could recognise my human attributes, which allowed her to treat me with the respect that all humans deserved. On that principle she asked me to please leave her door immediately. I politely complied. Another middle-class voter enquired about the party's policy on atheism. I pointed out that atheism didn't yet animate the imaginations of the average voter. Several middle-class voters said they would support us because their kids were in school with the children of my candidate. Another middle-class concern was the threat to the mandatory status of the Irish language in secondary schools. I tried hard to resist telling them about the effect Peig Sayers has had on me. I didn't mention Peig in the national interest. I had learned at orientation that the golden rule of canvassing is that you should not argue with the voter. I quickly moved on to the next door, promising myself I would go to see my analyst soon.

A sign on a door read:

> *No leaflets. No menus. No ads. No flyers. No business cards. No political pamphlets. No campaigners.*
> *We do not donate to charities that call to the door. We do not buy things at the door.*
> *We do not vote for anyone at the door.*
> *(And no – we do not need or want TV or telephones. We are entirely self-sufficient).*

I knocked on a battered brown door. The little old man beckoned me into his hall with his index finger while nervously looking up and down the street. 'Is there anyone out there with you?' he asked, peeking over my shoulder.

'No. It's just me,' I lied.

'When C was here yesterday, I swear I saw our ex-Taoiseach hiding in that bush over there. Do you think I'm cracking up or what? Is it possible I saw him?'

'Anything is possible,' I said.

'I'm probably all right but at my age it's hard to tell.'

At a red door the man who opened it stared quizzically at me before shrugging and saying 'I no speak English, you know?'

I tell him that I am sorry for disturbing his telly watching. As I turn away, a voice from inside shouts, 'Who's that luv?'

He replies, 'Just some fucking canvasser' before closing the door.

At a green door I was told, '*Your candidate* promised me a pedestrian crossing at the bottom of the road for the children coming from school. My son was in primary school then. Now he's in secondary but I think he will be at university by the time we get it.' The green door closed.

At another green door an old woman points at a framed portrait of Michael Collins on the wall in the hallway of her home. The picture has a small light burning beneath it which it shares with the Sacred Heart picture beside it, and both are surrounded by fresh flowers. She smiles and gives me a thumbs-up sign before gently closing the door.

Later, at a white door, I am asked if my candidate can work miracles.

'Yes he can,' I said confidently. 'He can actually work miracles.'

'I'll probably vote for him so.' The white door closed.

I met the rest of my canvassing pack at an intersection of two residential roads. They were taking a fag break while discussing the performance of *our candidate* earlier on national television.

'I thought Pablo got a dig in. Do you think he got a dig in? I think he really got a dig in!'

Meanwhile, a van pulled up. Four men dressed in black got out with a short ladder. They started to take down a poster from a nearby telephone pole.

'Is that one of our posters?' a pack member asked about the placard being stashed in the back of the van.

'No, it's one of them.'

'That's okay so! As I was saying, he got a real dig in at your man.' Fags finished, we started down another road with our pack leader shouting after us: 'Remember lads. Ninety seconds max per door and don't argue with the punters.'

The Rules of Guessing

When canvassing in the mornings, you are most likely to meet people who work the night shift trying to sleep. If they do get up out of bed to open the door, you will wish they hadn't. You meet the unemployed, if they haven't left the house to lie on the canal bank and feed the ducks. You also meet the retired, who like to discuss their frailties with anyone who calls to their door.

'Do you have any questions?' Pablo asked an elderly man on the East Wall.

'Do you have a cure for arthritis?' the old man asked in earnest.

I discovered that I don't have a face for politics: apparently my expressions seem to betray my inner emotions. I found this out many times but especially during the voter guessing game. A custom of canvassing the older voter is that, before you elicit any specific details, you are invited to guess what that information is. On a cold and rainy morning, I was standing half way down a path, dripping wet and waiting for a pause in the conversation that would allow me to drag Pablo away from an elderly woman who had developed guessing to a refined art. She had been discoursing on her illnesses and diagnoses for ten minutes.

'What age do you think I am? Guess. What age?' she asked, pointing to her chest.

'Seventy-nine,' Pablo said, while I said 'Fifty' on the principle that you should always flatter a woman about her age.

'Fifty? Fifty! Will you go away with your fifty? I'm sixty-eight.'

I felt more diplomatic than Pablo; I thought I felt more political. Pablo could learn something from me. Having allowed myself to be drawn into the guessing game, she was next asking us to guess how many illnesses she had in the last year. 'Five,' I guessed, while Pablo offered nine. 'Twelve,' she said with pride, happy to have out-foxed us. Warming up, she asked us to guess how many times she had been in hospital. 'Twelve,' I said, immediately getting into the logic of the competition, while Pablo guessed nine again. Afterwards I asked him if nine was his lucky number.

'No,' he said, 'I always guess nine. Why not?'

Back at the contest she told us smugly that she had been in hospital fifteen times. I was still doing the mental arithmetic to work out the frequency of her visits when she asked us to guess how much she had spent on pills in the last year alone. Pablo tried nine thousand euro, while I suggested a million under my breath.

'Two thousand,' she told us. Disappointed, she pointed at me and said to Pablo, 'Look at him. He's standing there smiling at me. Thank God for you, Pablo. I'll vote for you. I won't vote for him.' Unlike me, Pablo is able to keep the smile at bay when he has to.

The Rules of Asking Questions

If you have no interest in either a candidate or their policies and if you don't want them to be elected, you should draw up a list of at least ten questions with which to ambush them when they knock on your door. Better still, invite the candidate you don't want to be elected into your kitchen for tea and biscuits. Then unroll your scroll of questions. My candidate, Pablo, a member of a conservative party, was invited into the kitchen of two lesbian voters. We knew they were lesbians because they announced this fact first thing when they opened their door together: 'Hi. We're lesbian voters.'

The day before, the party leader had announced that his party would not be supporting gay marriage but would be supporting stag hunting, as befits a conservative manifesto. Pablo had received an avalanche of tweets from gay and animal rights voters from all over the country who pledged never to vote for him in a million elections.

After passing round the tea and plates of biscuits, they began the interrogation. One, putting on her reading glasses, started at the top of her list. 'Why is your party against gay marriage?' she asked, while holding hands with the other.

'Do you know anything about our party?' Pablo asked. 'We don't support gay marriage because we are a conservative party serving a conservative demographic. Perhaps you should vote for any of the liberal parties. I can say with confidence that our party leader, if elected, won't be entering into a gay marriage during the lifetime of the next government.' The tea came down my nose.

'What about the poor stags? What have they ever done to you?' the other one asked. It had started to rain outside so I was happy to stay in that warm kitchen for another hour, which was how long it took to get through the questions.

Another morning, I sat at the back of Fourth Class in St Laurence O'Toole's Junior Boys' School just off Sheriff Street, where the main candidates in the constituency were holding a question-and-answer session with the boys. The boys meant business because they started the debate by gathering together in the middle of the classroom for a Māori haka.

The first question was, 'Mary Lou? What will you do about the (dog) poo?'

Dog references were common on the campaign, with recommendations that the tail stop wagging the dog; how knowledgeable the dogs on the street were about precisely what was going on in politics in Ireland; how closely the life of a dog resembled that of a politician; how certain politicians were barking up the wrong trees, while making a dog's dinner of the economy in general; and how many candidates wasted their time chewing on the same old bones.

Mary Lou gave the questioner ten out of ten for poetry. I was impressed with the rest of the questions but they didn't rhyme. The toughest audience I had seen so far.

After a month of campaigning, headquarters looked like a military control centre on the wrong side in a major conflict. Unused posters were stacked in leaning towers. Weeks of newspapers that had been analysed for the smallest hints of voting trends lay where they had fallen on desks. Waste bins overflowed with demolished fast-food wrappers. Coats lay like dead bodies on the floor. The number of desks had increased with the number of phones, along with the number of those constantly relaying messages and instructions on them. There were five large maps of the constituency pasted to the wall, with different titles on each. One indicated the location of posters, another the streets to which leaflets had been dropped, another the End of Term Report Card[23] distribution and another the streets to which the Five Point Plan had been delivered. On the fifth map, the largest, in a variety of colours, the rate of progress of the actual canvassing was highlighted. With one day left to the election, I would not have been surprised to find a monocled general waving a baton in front of any of these maps. All the streets had been coloured in with pink, blue or green highlighter pen. All was quiet on the Central Front as the canvassers were taking a very rare few moments to themselves, when the door opened and a complete stranger walked in. She asked no one in particular whom she should talk to in order to get her medical card sorted. We all pointed at R. While looking in the general direction of R, she loudly told all of us her gynaecological history, much of which was too technical for us to appreciate without medical qualifications. Someone picked up a pile of Five Point Plans, suggesting that we all head out to pick up the few remaining houses. There was a rush for the door. No one had cars so we took taxis to the front lines. I was reminded of the fighters in Madrid in the Spanish Civil War.

The Old Lady Rules

Most of the elderly female constituents have tiny dogs that bark while jumping up and down on the windowsill between the lace curtains and the glass. They are well practised at baring their teeth in a convincing demonstration of their horrible nasty little personalities. In dog language

---

[23] This was the name that the campaign gave to a flyer detailing Pablo's (political) achievements to date.

they are saying, 'Look at me, look at me. She loves me and doesn't care that I am such a little shit.' I have a theory about these dogs. When their owners were young they hoped to fall in love with, and marry, criminally insane bad boys who would treat them terribly and make their lives a delicious drama of thoughtless agonies. Instead, they settled for responsible, hard-working sensible husbands who were fine but dull. They really wanted dull but liked to imagine they were into pain. When their faithful husbands expired, they decided to live out their early dreams of the wild life with these hairy little monsters. They come in a variety of degrees of hairiness and they are everywhere. These self-satisfied three-inch mutts specialise in biting your fingertips when you put flyers through the letterbox four feet from the ground. I imagine they have little trampolines set up inside the doors. Bastards. Smug little hairy bastards. But you should call to their houses because the votes of their owners are important. As you stand there with your fingers dripping blood, the little old lady says, hugging the grinning, mangy vampiric ball of fleas to her bosom, 'Oh has little Fluffy Poo been naughty? Bad Fluffy Poo.' Then she starts kissing Fluffy Poo! For the sake of the party you say, 'Not at all' and you risk your remaining good fingers by patting Fluffy Poo on the head.

You should canvas in the rain because old ladies then take pity on you. Pablo told me that during the previous election an old lady approached him on the street on the day of voting to remind him that he had called round to her door in the pouring rain, and just for that she was going to give him her number one. I decided to try this myself. After waiting for a downpour, I headed out to a small circle of cottages that formed sheltered housing for the elderly. I felt confident I would meet a few sympathetic old dears there. I knocked loudly at the first door and waited a few minutes. Imagining that the old lady I had in mind wouldn't be running to the door, I decided to wait at least two more minutes. I thought that perhaps she might be hard of hearing so I knocked again, this time loudly. I waited another minute. Just then the rain stopped, so I was losing interest in my anthropological experiment. As I turned to go, I heard a bolt being opened on the other side of the door, then another, another, a catch, a chain and another bolt. The unbolting went on for three minutes. At last a crack appeared through which I could just see my little old lady – sitting in a wheelchair. I felt guilty for making her go to such efforts for my cynical trial. I delivered my spiel in a half-hearted way. Then she opened the door and asked me if I wanted to come in out of the rain because I must be soaking. I was wondering what the point was in having fifty bolts on your door if you invited complete strangers inside.

She advised me: 'What ye need is some joined-up thinking. For that you need one huge computer and not just a lot of smaller ones. With one enormous computer you could have all the information on everyone in the one place. That way there would be no messing.'

I promised to pass on her advice to technical headquarters, wondering if perhaps, when younger, she had been in the cast of a Bond film.

The Rules of Voting

At last the morning of the vote arrived. I was happy because I was exhausted from following my research from door to door for a month. As the slogan says, 'Vote early and vote often', so I headed down to the voting station in the local primary school to cast my fifteen votes. This is not just voting. This is the *proportional representation single transferrable vote system.* There are a few simple rules involved. The easiest way to understand our voting system is to take a degree in political science. Failing that, imagine the following: there are fifteen candidates belonging to a variety of major parties or independent agendas running for election in a four-seat constituency. For example, let's say that there are four parties each running two candidates and two other parties running one candidate each, plus five independents. What should you as the voter do in this case?

Totally naive people, or foreign correspondents, imagine that you are supposed to put a number on the ballot paper from one to fifteen beside each candidate's name in order of your preference. Not so. Irish voters know how the system works. You should put a '1' beside the name of the candidate who you believe is going to top the poll rather than the candidate who you necessarily want to top the poll. This information is available from Paddy Power Bookmakers prior to Election Day. This means that when that candidate is elected, your vote will transfer to another candidate as a proportion of their surplus so you will get to vote twice, in effect. Next, turn to the bottom of the list and, working backwards, place a '15' beside the candidate that Paddy Power tells you has no hope whatsoever. You should do this even if you are related to that candidate. Follow the same method for fourteen through to eleven. You now have just nine numbers left. At this point it begins to get complicated, but don't panic. If Paddy Power has a clear second favourite, you can feel confident in putting a '2' beside that name. Again your vote will transfer to the next candidate, proportionally if not actually, but you never can tell so don't worry about it. You just have to think positively. Do this for not more than three candidates in a four-seat constituency and for not more than four candidates in a five-seater. Subsequently, you should vote for the candidate who you actually want to see elected. Then give your number ten to their main competitor for the seat. Fill in the other numbers according to how the candidates look in their photographs on the ballot paper. My assumption is that you won't want to vote for the most popular candidate because that is less challenging to your democratic principles or you are not the kind to follow the herd. I am also assuming that you will want to be directly involved in electing all four candidates. It is such a simple system I can't understand why so many voters find it confusing. I don't know why every country in the world doesn't use it. The *first past the post system* in a single-seat constituency is just so boring. Anyone could manage to vote in a system like that. In our system we never know what is going to happen until the oracle that is Paddy Power has spoken. And the people of course. Let's not forget the people. I voted. Following the principles of PR-STV voting, I gave Pablo my number one because Paddy Power said he was the favourite.

The Tally

In order to complete my embedded role with Fine Gael and achieve methodological closure, I begged the cumann chairman to allow me to attend the count as a tallyman. A tallyman is the prophet to whom the media refer in all their coverage of the election results. The tallyman knows before anyone else, except Paddy Power, who is going to be elected.

7.15 a.m.: You should know how to dress for a count. When I arrived at headquarters, hi-viz jackets were being handed out emblazoned with the name of our candidate on the back. One of our tallywomen refused to put it on, claiming that yellow did nothing for her. Apparently they were the exact same shade as the bridesmaid's dress she was forced to wear to her sister's wedding. 'I swore then I would never wear yellow again.' The rest of us, indifferent to our sartorial elegance, climbed into the back of a white van like a road repair crew in search of a pothole.

8.15 a.m.: You should bring a computer with you. When we arrived outside the Royal Dublin Showgrounds, the security man at the door asked the people operating computers to make their way inside first, but he couldn't be heard above the noise of the growing crowd of tallymen and general hangers-on. Someone in the crowd shouted loudly, 'Nerds! Nerds! The man is looking for the nerds. If you're a nerd make your way inside now. Nerds to the front.' A half dozen nerds proudly marched into the RDS, waving their laptops at security as proof of their nerdiness.

8.30 a.m.: When we got inside, we ran to our allocated few feet of railing to await the start of the count. The counters hadn't arrived yet. A party of Fianna Fáil supporters passed by carrying a huge hamper of food. When they saw me looking enviously at their supplies, they shouted over to me that because there was going to be a 'dog fight' it was best to come prepared. Seeing my FG jacket, one of them asked me if I was a die-hard Blueshirt.[24] I told them that I was not. Then they asked if I was even 'gene-pool Fine Gael'. I also denied this.

---

[24] In the 1930s the prominent Irish politician Eoin O'Duffy was so taken with fascism that, when he became leader of the Army Comrades Association, he changed their name to the National Guard and adopted many of cutting-edge fascist behaviours that were fashionable across Europe at that time. Amongst others, these included the Roman salute and a sartorial obsession with shirt wearing. In Germany, the preferred shirt colour was brown, while in England and Italy it was black. O'Duffy, making a fashion statement of his own, made his followers wear blue. They quickly became known as the Blueshirts. In 1933, Cumann na nGaedheal, the Centre Party and the National Guard (aka the Blueshirts) merged to form Fine Gael under the leadership of O'Duffy. I am not saying that they were a fascist organisation but everyone else seemed to think so. By the 1970s, Blueshirt had become the nickname for Fine Gael.

'Anyway come over at lunchtime for a sandwich. We have loads.'

9.10 a.m.: The point in tallying is to write down all the number one votes for each candidate. Each box of the one hundred and four boxes was emptied in turn onto the counting tables in front of the railings to which the tallypersons were attached. The votes were opened out and flattened into two piles by two counters. A tallyperson was assigned to each pile. They called the vote preferences to a partner who marked them off on a sheet containing the box numbers. The nerds, who were in a special nerd coral, in turn tallied all the sheets. The idea was that the tallypeople, who made all the complex calculations, would know who was going to be elected moments before everyone else.

Where the tallyperson is most powerful is in predicting the outcome of the tenth plus count that would happen in the middle of the next night. For this, you need to memorise the pattern of transfers from candidates who you know will be eliminated from the first box, and the next and the next, for all fifteen candidates. No problem!

There is an art to spoiling your vote. Someone had voted for candidates in the order 1, 2, 3, 4, cunt, 5, 6, 7, etc. We wondered if that would count. We decided to include it in our tally. Someone else had written a single word beside each candidate to form the fifteen-word sentence: 'Mickey Mouse, Minnie Mouse and Donald Duck could do a better job than this shower.'

A tallyman, who I subsequently discovered had been tallying for fifty-six years, pushed his way to the railing to check how we were doing.

'Keep your fecking eyes on the score lads. A crowd of fecking eejits over there in yellow jackets are after making a complete haimes of two boxes so our numbers are going to be completely thrown out.'

10.00 a.m.: You should try to know what is happening seconds before anyone else. On our first break someone passing shouted at no one in particular, '_____ is gone. Dead in the water already.'

'Jaysus,' one of us said in response, 'any other big scalps?'

'Not yet.'

There was a general happiness at the bad news and delight to have been amongst the first to hear it.

10.15 a.m.: You should listen to the roaring of the crowd. 'What's happened?' I asked after being deafened by a thunderous shout.

'_____ is gone!'

'Already? No way. That's amazing.'

The yell marked the end of an illustrious political career.

11.00 a.m.: Attach yourself to someone who knows what they are doing. I was being an apprentice to the highly experienced tallyman. He was conscientiously taking me through the numbers for our candidates after 40 per cent of the boxes had been opened. Pointing at columns of numbers beside each candidate's name, he told me that he 'wants to get him out, do you see? When he is gone his votes will transfer to her, but that might not be in time to save her there. But if I get rid of him and him – but their votes could go anywhere – I might be able to get him in.'

'What are you saying?' I asked.

He sighed with contempt at my ignorance, repeating for the third time a variation of how he willed the votes to go.

'So you are saying he will win,' I said, pointing to a no-hoper.

'Christ almighty. What kind of fucking eejits are they letting in here these days? These are the four that are going to win in this order.'

'Are you sure?' I asked, curious to see how red he could become.

'Yes, I am fucking sure. I have been doing this for fucking fifty-six fucking years.'

He stalked off, looking, I thought, for a quiet corner in which to have a stroke. I rejoined my hi-viz colleagues to tell them that I had worked out, all by myself, who was going to win the seats in our constituency and in what order. They told me I hadn't a clue.

11.30 a.m.: When you think you have vital information, pass it on immediately. I met a journalist I know from *The Guardian* who asked me if I knew who was going to win. It had to be the jacket: the jacket of knowledge. I told him I was certain of the result at this stage. He took notes and hurried off. When you wear a hi-viz jacket, people think you know things like where the toilets are, who is ahead in the count, what did your man say, where can you get a coffee, who will win and what the quota is. I pointed out directions to obscure places, gave the first name that came into my mind and threw out any numbers that seemed plausible within three decimal places. I had become an info-maniac.

11.50 a.m.: When you are recognised as a prophet, you should try to profit from it. A fellow vizzer approached to apologise for his earlier outburst of abuse at my predictions. It seems that I was right all along because he just got the same view on his iPhone from *The Guardian* website.

12.30 p.m.: You should attach yourself to someone with better sandwiches than you.

'Who has the hang?'[25] someone in a hi-viz jacket asked. 'I can't believe it. No one brought a fecking hang sandwich.'

---

[25] Hang is Hiberno-English for ham. Hang is probably the most popular sandwich filling, followed closely by hang and cheese,

You should talk about the candidates as if they are all in an intensive care unit. Over grub we discussed those who 'still have a pulse'. A candidate with barely a pulse passed by.

'Did you hear how ___ is doing?'

'Still hanging in there.'

'I hear the Green is going well.'

'He conceded defeat two hours ago.'

After another collective shout, we heard that M was gone at a distant counting island in the far corner of the hall.

'Is she really gone? I can't believe it.'

'She still has a pulse but it's very faint.'

'You know what lost it for her? It was the hair! It was her hair that lost it for her!'

'Do you not think it was her fourteen years in government and the mess she made of everything?'

'No, it was the hair. Did you see the hair on her?'

'Hair or no hair, it's touch and go with her now. It could go either way. She's not expected to make it. The prognosis is very poor. We should prepare ourselves for the worst.'

1.00 p.m.: A vizzer rushed to tell me that Pablo, who was heading the poll, had arrived outside because they were about to announce the vote. We gathered outside in a highly luminous circle around the taxi to carry Pablo inside. The first count had ended so they were ready to announce the winner, Pablo. Our campaign manager started crying.

---

stuffed chicken, banana and egg salad. While many sandwich bars have sprung up all over the country, using a wide variety of fancy brown and white breads and a myriad of fillings, the authentic traditional Irish sandwich is hang on white sliced bread, preferably flattened in tin foil because you have kept it in your arse pocket. Unlike me on this occasion, you shouldn't go far from home without a hang sandwich, because sharing them is an important Irish social ritual.

3.20 p.m.: TV3 ordered pizza to form the centrepiece of a photo shoot with Pablo and his family sitting together eating. The assistant spread five boxes of pizza on the table and went away to find the camera crew. She returned two minutes later to find the camp followers of Fianna Fáil, Sinn Féin and the Greens finishing off the last few slices of Pablo's domestic prop. She retrieved one half-eaten slice for Pablo, who had his photo op in front of a table of empty boxes. Later, we had photos of Pablo on the phone looking business-like, Pablo stirring tea wisely, and Pablo walking without assistance and even talking at the same time.

4.10 p.m.: Bring your knitting with you to a count. Nothing happened for an hour. We clung to the railings and tried to sleep. A woman hanging beside me told me why she voted for a particular candidate. The story took fifty minutes. It involved a car crash, a fight, two trips to the hospital, a psychiatrist, an accountant, someone who worked in a hotel and a life-changing experience at Lourdes.

6.00 p.m.: Bring a sleeping bag with you to a count. A shout woke us as we were hanging on the rails like bats.
'The mammy of the Dáil is gone,' someone listening intently on their earpiece told us.
'Why did she run? Sure she must be a hundred.'
'Well, whatever age she is, she's gone now.'
The news of someone's misery causes happiness all round.

6.30 p.m.: If you are a candidate, don't turn up at a count unless you got at least fifty votes. Those who 'were gone' had quietly gone home; the very unpopular hadn't even turned up; those who were expected to be popular but weren't had gone home in shock. Those who were left were either the winners or the middle-ranking, nail-bitingly close competitors in the dog fight predicted to break out at around 1.00 a.m. By now we were waiting for transfers.

'We won't get anything off those independent lunatics. We'll have to go again. We'll be here all night,' someone said.

Almost immediately the word went round from the tally-people that Pablo had thirty votes from 'your man with the eyes'.

8.50 p.m.: You should work out if you are campaigning with a candidate who might win.

'Okay lads, we are ready to go. Get Pablo and bring him up front with the family. The TV cameras are ready for us. Who is going to hoist him up? The four of ye look the strong-est. Get in beside him. When I give the signal, throw him up in the air.'

The four who were nominated the most muscular had a tight hold on Pablo's arms and legs, ready to recklessly fling him into the air in traditional fashion.

One candidate got twenty-five votes. A security man standing beside me asked no one in particular whether or not that fecking eejit had any family.

'Wouldn't you think they would have voted for him. Must be some dangerous fecking loony if he can't get more than twenty-five votes out of his family and neighbours. Sure if he had hired a bus he would have done better than that. What kind of a person can't get more than twenty-five votes? Was he in jail or what during the campaign?'

9.00 p.m.: Don't drop your victorious candidate on national television. We threw Pablo into the air. The campaign manager cried more than everyone else put together.

'Right lads,' someone says, 'across the road en masse to the pub and don't put him down.'

They carried Pablo out of the building. My tally guru told me that Pablo's result wasn't too bad.

'It only took twelve hours. If those fecking eejits hadn't lost those twenty-five votes he would have been out of here ages ago.'

Ah, sweet victory! *My candidate* had been elected. In a good mood I returned to a nail-biting M still hanging on the railings. I told her that it was a scientific fact of tallying that she was going to win, despite my tally guru – who is never wrong – telling me she was going to lose. Why spread misery, I asked myself.

'Any hang sandwiches left?' I asked. She did lose just before 2.00 a.m.

1.55 a.m.: You should try to get some sleep. I was awoken hanging on the barrier to the shouts of the final candidate being carried around the end of the hall and out the door. My tally guru had got it right at 10.15 a.m. the previous day.

Some party high-ups thought that my going undercover with Fine Gael as a campaigner was so successful that they asked me to join the party. This was while I was at a victory celebration with free booze. As a general principle, it is not a good idea to ask me anything serious at a free bar. I am sure that a public apology may be required on my part if I could remember what I said while declining the offer. I vaguely recall mentioning my preferences for nailing my feet to the floor, etc., which was very ungracious behaviour towards some of the most gratuitously helpful people I have come across. My claims to be utterly unsuitable for membership of a political party, which I believe I demonstrated in the most unambiguous way at the party piss-up, were tolerantly ignored. I am not really a joiner. I don't even have a Tesco Clubcard. I prefer to watch us making fools of ourselves, though I frequently do participate at that level myself.

Once elected, you will be called upon to do favours for all of the people who participated in your campaign. This number will usually exceed the number of those who actually campaigned for you by a factor of ten. Now I have to work out what Pablo can do for me. Just yesterday I saw a dog pissing against a newly planted tree at the end of our street. Intolerable behaviour really. I will have to get on to Pablo about it.

* * *

While campaigning, I came across an old lady who lives alone in Glasnevin in the middle of a bustling neighbourhood. She invited me in and insisted I sit on her antique sofa in her tiny sitting room. She told me that she was eighty-nine years old and didn't have long to live because she had been diagnosed with cancer, for which she was receiving chemotherapy. She sat regally on the sofa, balancing a very unconvincing wig on her head that she must have last worn in the sixties when platinum beehives were the rage. I assumed it had been rightly banished to a shoebox in the back of her wardrobe sometime in the early seventies. She told me that she saw no one from one end of the day to the other. She insisted on my staying for tea, which I made in the enormous tea pot in the kitchen, and we talked about life and shite in general for half an hour.

10

Being Cool: Bono Who?

1-5 to 0-8...well, from Lapland to the Antarctic,
that's level scores in any man's language.

(Mícheál O'Muircheartaigh)

It is time to introduce some anthropological theory. One
of my favourite theorists, Claude Lévi-Strauss, developed
structural anthropology which, in part, compares binary
opposites such as culture/nature; raw/cooked; man/
woman; savage/civilised; sacred/profane. Structuralism
supposes that these kinds of oppositions are fundamental to
all language and thought, and that they are a basic tool for
organising culture and language. Fortunately, Irish culture
has many binary opposites worth examining. For example,
Dublin City provides us with a popular opposition between
Northsiders, who are all treated as savages, and *Southsiders*,
who are all viewed as civilised. The River Liffey defines the
border between these two distinct cultures. But all Dublin
City dwellers come together to share the cultural burden of
having to be cool when they are set opposite to all country
folk, who have to be sporty. This is probably why there are
really only two GAA football teams in Ireland: Dublin and

Anywhere But Dublin. For the sake of structuralists everywhere, I am happy to keep these tensions going by setting
the city against the country, the cool against the uncool and
the sedentary against the sporty. Structuralists don't judge
one side of these oppositions as being better than the other;
they believe that each gets its meaning and energy from the
rivalry.

Every contemporary culture has its ways of being cool,
just like everyone in Ireland has a Bono[26] story. There are
definite things you can do to become an icon of hip urbanity.
There are rules you can follow on how to become cool. These
are the rules Bono didn't follow (what's with those glasses?).
I have discovered during my research on cool people that no
one wants to be Bono. In the words my coolest informant –
'Who is Bono?'

Classic structuralist anthropology uses comparative analysis to help illustrate behaviour. Anthropology is cool because
you can hang out with cool people. It's also uncool when
you have to hang out with uncool people. I just have to be
myself. By looking at aspects of both, I will compare the cool
with the uncool. The frenetic life of the urbane hipster is
distinct from the fusty existence of the rural GAA fan.

An anthropology of Irish behaviour is not complete
without including some sporting activities. Sport is hugely
important in Ireland. It takes very many forms, from GAA
hurling and football to tennis, golf, soccer, rugby, drifting,
swimming, athletics, horse racing, dog racing and racing
anything, including bikes, hamsters, cars and trucks. On any
Monday our newspapers are filled with reports of the weekend sporting events. Sports are important to anthropology
because they have very many social effects. For example,
'avoiding the match on the telly' provides Irish women with
an excuse to go shopping; anything racing on wheels or legs

---

[26] It is vital that you pronounce this name correctly – 'Bow-No'.

provides an opportunity to go to the bookmakers to bet on 'two flies crawling up a wall'; and participating in GAA sports allows us to express our inner uncool selves.

Being uncool is important because it helps us to define its opposite, being cool, which in Ireland can often be measured by how far removed from the GAA you are. These states have to be studied together as complementary behaviours. To follow sports, you need to be part of a mob. But to be cool is to be individual and shun the crowd. Anthropology studies popular culture, even where that popular culture involves the effort to be as unpopular as possible.

* * *

There is an intrinsic difficulty in researching cutting-edge habits. The shelf-life of the behaviours in question is so necessarily short that, by the time they get into print, they should be passé. Therefore, my writing about what is happening now in Ireland is more a nostalgia piece because the venues, clothes and behaviours that support what is *so now* should be *so over* by the time you are reading this. In contrast, the wonderful thing about the GAA is that it changes, if at all, very, very slowly. It prides itself on its conservatism, which is what makes it, by definition, so uncool.

Avant-garde trends constantly replace themselves. Being up-to-the-minute is a phase that we should all try to go through at least once, because being cool is an essential stage of our individual cultural engagement. Every contemporary society has a sub-group whose function it is to set that society's standards in what counts as fashionable in clothes, music and art, and what ideas to espouse as being *so now* and what ones to abandon as being *so over*. That job is practically a full-time career for those who take on the responsibility. To do it well, it is necessary to have just enough money to support your signature lifestyle. But you shouldn't get your money from employment, which can be a distraction from your responsibility to trends. You need to be just poor enough to be earnest about making a difference in the world and rich enough to be able to acquire the trappings of being socially cool. When you are too rich, you move out to uncool suburban havens for the uncooly successful or even into castles, like some of our stars. Being cool in Ireland is a fine balancing act between the gauche extremes of poverty and wealth.

If you are urban based and unemployed after spending seven years – finger quotation signs in the air – 'studying' Music Technology, and you are just too self-aware to scream your head off and drench your fellow fans with spittle at a GAA match, you will need to find comfort in the company of other like-minded people.

Where to Stay Cool

An initial search for cool people took me to Trinity College, or *Trinners,* because an informant told me that he once saw some cool people there. They may have been tourists; he wasn't certain. But we agreed it was a starting place for my research. Some students are cool, but, for the sake of demographic rigour, I am not including students who actually attend lectures, even in a sporadic way, under the category of hip people. However, there is a grey area between, on the one hand, students who are on campus every day attending class, going to the library and actually studying, and those who are technically registered as students. No one amongst the former group can qualify as cool. Some among the latter may. The first step in becoming cool is to register as a student. But you are not yet cool. The second step is to register in the right college. How cool you can potentially be is directly related to where you are registered. Trinity is very cool, but only if you are studying Literature, Music,

Media and Sound Engineering. History can be cool but it depends on what area you are pretending to study. Military history is cool. You might get away with Psychology but you'd probably be pushing it. It is also cool to be registered in the National College of Art and Design and some schools in Dublin Institute of Technology, but it is not cool to be registered in University College Dublin. Maynooth is totally uncool. In general, undergraduates are not cool. Some are definitely uncool because they live at home in Naas and commute to a course in Applied Technology in UCD. They also play Gaelic in the evenings with Grangenolvin Football Club. After graduating somehow, following the third step to coolness, register on a postgraduate course. By following these three steps you will achieve the minimum qualifications for consideration as being possibly hip.

And for God's sake, don't turn up to lectures. How uncool! Do turn up for the first lecture to pick up the syllabus and reading list, in order to be aware of what you are missing and the books you should be reading. The Greek philosopher Socrates was the first person to point out the vital epistemological difference, well understood today by hip people, between knowing what you don't know – which you will know by attending not more than three lectures – and *not* knowing what you don't know – which you will not know if you don't turn up at all. The former state of being is cool. The latter is not. You might also attend all the lectures only if you are thick. That might be cool in certain circumstances because it is not always cool to exclude thick people. You will need to offer both yourself and your friends convincing excuses for not attending class, because you should pretend to everyone, including yourself, that you care. One of the best excuses would be that your band rehearsals are clashing with lecture times. Another satisfactory excuse is that you were up all night puking from the sushi you had the evening before to celebrate completing your new one-minute-fifteen-second short film. Or how about you fell asleep on the train to Santiago Airport and didn't wake up until you got to Lisbon. If you want to take it to the limit of coolness, register for a postgraduate course in Sound Engineering in Trinners, turn up for one class, which will be enough to get a job for two hours per annum as a first-year tutor in jazz banjo in the National College of Art and Design, and then don't turn up for work.

If you want to be cool, you have to be able to at least recognise the difference between being an undergraduate student, which is not cool; being a graduate student who attends lectures in a prosaic topic such as Accounting or Law, which is also not cool; and being in the seventh year of your MA in Experimental Music and Development Studies at Trinners, where you have completed two field trips exploring the therapeutic value of bongo rhythms amongst HIV populations in Laos, but have not actually attended any lectures, which is very cool. If you are an undergraduate student, you may live in student accommodation, which is extremely uncool, but not as uncool as living at home with your parents, which is actually even less cool than becoming a hurler on a GAA team. If you have any potential for hipness, by the time you have gotten into third year, you should have moved into an apartment in Rathmines with three other students. If you are studying something uncool, use the opportunity to move in with students who are studying cool subjects such as Philosophy, Theology or even Classics. When you graduate to be officially unemployed and your parents refuse to pay for the apartment you saw in Ranelagh, you should move into a tiny cottage down a back alley in Dublin 8 with your new cool partner who you've met at a non-competitive film festival at the Irish Film Institute in Temple Bar. If you are both rich and cool, you may be able to afford an alley in Dublin 6W.

No matter how bad things get, you should never exchange your Southside alley for one on the Northside. No one living on the Northside is cool. You may visit Stoneybatter to eat sparingly, drink moderately, or even attend an underground art show, but you should get back over the river before dawn. There is a hard-core enclave of people living in Great Western Square in Phibsborough who think they are cool, and a few sprinkled around Drumcondra and Stoneybatter. But otherwise the Northside is a hip-free zone. Remember, there are no cool people living outside Dublin. Cork? Let's not go there, unless you can get to the English Market without passing through the city.

The Rules of Looking Cool

There are a few simple things you can do to look cool. You can carry cool stuff. In anthropology, the effect of taking on the nature of something through contact is called *contagious magic*. Carrying a violin case is cool. Carrying a cello or banjo case is cooler. Carrying a double base case is the coolest. You will get away with a saxophone case but leave the guitar case at home.

When not practising the magic of carrying cool stuff, try looking cool. To look cool in Dublin you have to be thin. This is true if you are either male or female. Dieting is helped if you have no money for food. Being unemployed in something cool in media helps with having no money. In any case, you shouldn't be seen dead in McDonald's scoffing burgers even when coked out of your head. No matter how stoned you are, remember no cool person would be so stoned as to wander into McDonald's. In fact, you wouldn't even protest outside McDonald's against the carbon footprint of their large fries.

You should have a cool day. When you are awoken in your alley in Dublin 8 or 6W at 11.15 a.m. by the sound of your totally uncool neighbour galloping by your window on a piebald pony, you should stagger into your kitchenette to brew your first coffee of the day. Coffee and cigarettes are the ideal breakfast for the cool thin person, but it is essential to only drink ethical fair trade coffee. It often costs less than unfair trade coffee. Before you can go outside, you have to dress appropriately. Males should get their skinny legs into skinny jeans, a horizontally striped top with mismatching striped cardigan and a leather jacket that you imagine Joey Ramone once wore. This will also work for females, but they could also wear a floral-print or polka dot vintage dress with ballet-pump shoes. In summer, males can wear sports sandals that, with obvious irony, have nothing sporty about them. Females can wear flip-flops. If you run out of clothes or olives, go to the Georges St Arcade to pick up some environmentally sound pre-loved outfits. In winter, if you need to go out, place a layer of newspapers under your summer outfits. But if you have heating don't go out. If you are not seen for three months, tell your friends that you over-wintered in Biarritz.

The Rules of Economic Inactivity

If you want to be cool you are allowed to be *economically inactive* but not unemployed. The difference is not well understood by those from the countryside, but it is important. It is possible to be economically inactive in a variety of ways, while there is only one way to be unemployed. Seasonal lecturing is a grey area because many people who – finger quotation signs in the air – "teach" sign on the dole during the summer. But you are allowed to do that and remain cool. There are several common forms of economic inactivity.

Writing a PhD is a form of economic inactivity, as is pursuing any form of research, including not turning up for lectures on your taught master's course. Being a sole trader is an easy path to economic inactivity. You can be inactive as a web designer, animator, journalist, anything graphical or musical, or by owning your own pop-up food or clothes shop that you should run in a fashion designed to be unsuccessful. In your pop-up shop you will quickly see the practical advantages of not studying either Business or Accounting as an undergraduate. Having a qualification in multimedia, as opposed to just one medium, will enhance your chances of becoming economically inactive.

While in this precise economic condition, you can apply for funding from a variety of sources: tap your parents regularly for small amounts and threaten that you will emigrate if funds are not forthcoming; borrow money from your partner's wallet, man-bag or designer purse, because having separate bank accounts is so unromantic; participate in an obscure arts grant that one of your friends secured (remember to reciprocate); accidentally make a sale in your pop-up shop; smoke fags because they kill your appetite; do some – finger quotation signs in the air – "teaching" in Dublin Institute of Technology, which involves turning up to tell the uncool students actually in class how cool you are; play a gig in Whelan's on Wexford St, which will keep you going for ages; get your parents to give you your college fees upfront for seven years for your two-year course and only pay the registration fee;[27] design a website for your mate's band who just got a gig in Whelan's, which will keep you going for two and a half days.

---

[27] Do not explain to your parents that the difference between college fees and registration fees is about five thousand euro. There is no need for your parents to know who does and who doesn't have to pay fees. As far as they are concerned, you do pay fees. Anyway, it's not stealing. They had you – you didn't ask to be born.

The Rules of Dating Someone Cool

Almost as effective as carrying something cool is the tactic of dating someone who is already cool. All the coolest women have letters instead of names: AD, B, JJ, KA, PJ, JP, L and M. If you have an actual name, hopefully you are called after a Jane Austen character. I asked Emma, who is cool, if she would go on a date with Steve, who aspired to be cool, in the interest of social science. She was to report back to me on how it all went. I proposed to pay her expenses. As she was economically inactive, she had to accept. I told her to think of it as a form of grant. She got herself introduced to Steve through their mutual acquaintance D. Emma is a friend of D, who is a friend of JJ, who is registered on the same music course as Caroline. Caroline knows Steve.

After the initial introductions, they agreed to meet upstairs in the Working Man's Club, which is the most ironically named venue in Ireland. Emma has long red hair tied up in a bun with elastic bands. Not the kind of red hair that is often accompanied by large freckles but a more subtle unnatural red. On her research date she wore black plastic framed glasses, a genuine 1950s red peasant swing dress, imported from New York for her birthday by her friend Fanny, and red pumps. Over all this she wore her matching 1950s leather jacket. She wore a flower in her hair. She informed me that Steve wore a red and black striped cardigan that was two sizes two small for him, with skinny jeans and black runners with white soles. It was love at first sight.

Steve carried his ironically brick-sized S180 mobile phone with extra loud ringer and built-in hearing-aid function as well as his standard iPhone 4 for e-mail and web. Emma had an iPad. They immediately compared technologies by measuring site speed and resolutions. Up to that point, Emma swore to only use Apple technology rather than anything Android, because she was an economically inactive sound engineer ignoring her research into psychoacoustics specifically in wind instrument systems.[28] While not doing research, it is important not to do that research in a very well-defined topic, otherwise you might not be allowed to register for the programme. Steve and Emma sat together, gazing into each other's screens. He sipped a Black Russian while she sipped a Hendrick's gin and tonic with a slice of cucumber.

There was a very cool art exhibition hanging on the walls of the Working Man's Club of Lichtenstein-inspired paintings of mouthless women with automatic weapons. There was a very cool communications student on the music deck playing Smiths covers. Emma asked Steve to dance with the other cool people who were clutching bottles of Corona and making ironically bad dancing moves near their table. They danced together for three songs, developing a hybrid salsa-waltz move in the process.

He asked if he could take her to dinner and she agreed. They nervously walked northwards across the river to L Mulligan Grocer in Stoneybatter. To distract themselves from the local northside Neanderthals, they discussed their tastes in music, which was a subject really important to both of them. Steve told Emma that he plays a kena, which he explained is a bamboo flute played by the Quechua Indians of Peru and Bolivia, in a band that composes soundtracks for old episodes of *Hawaii Five-O*. He was embarrassed to admit that he actually learned to play a Korean twelve-string zither when he was studying philosophy at Trinners. She admitted that, while her very first instrument had been a Hohner accordion, she had moved on to the piano. Yes,

---

[28] Most Irish engineering students really want to be architects or designers, and everyone knows that Apple is the best platform for graphics. That is why the iPhone is the preferred smart phone of engineers.

while it was a mainstream instrument, it was amazing the sounds that could be gotten out of it by bashing the strings with a drumstick. While she was studying the psychoacoustic effects of wind instruments, she felt it was essential that you not get caught up in actually playing the instrument yourself. Therefore, it was best not to know how to play. Steve agreed. He admitted that the kena was endangering his real appreciation of music.

They moved on to discussing their favourite bands. They both believed that Florence and the Machine had absolutely sold out and gone mainstream, and that anyone appearing on *Later with Jools Holland* was a traitor to authentic music. Emma admitted to liking some mainstream bands like The Postal Service, Alex on Fire and Death Cab and, of course, As I Lay Dying. But Steve wasn't so sure. He preferred bands that laid down a few tracks for posterity and broke up on the same day as forming. He had been in three such bands and thought that at least they had set the benchmark for anti-commercial authenticity. But they could agree that, for those who are cool, music is not something you listen to – it is an accessory.

When they arrived in L Mulligan Grocer, they sat at a small table for two. He ordered a Schneider Tap 2 Weissbier and she had a glass of Belfast Blonde beer. The menus arrived buried in old hardback books. Studying these naturally led to a discussion of their eating habits. Emma told Steve that she was big into the *locavore* idea and tried to only eat in places that supported it. As a result, she didn't eat out very often. Maybe you are not cool enough to know that the locavore diet promotes a healthy planet by encouraging its followers to eat produce sourced within a ten-mile radius, which in practical terms covers all of Dublin 8. Before locavore, Emma was big into the Gourmet Burger explosion until the novelty wore off. She would now only consider Rick's Burgers on Dame Street to be authentic, while Jo'burger in

Ranelagh does cool chips. They found they shared a love of sushi and Asian food in general, but 'you can't get decent Asian in Dublin – everyone knows that.'

Steve told Emma that he was once a vegan who subsisted mainly on adzuki-bean burgers, but that now he was a strict vegetarian who sometimes ate fish, chicken, burgers, mince (only when it was really lean) and steaks (only when they were rare fillets), which he would only eat when visiting his parents every weekend.

Emma decided not to order anything and Steve ordered the bangers and mash. While they waited for the food to arrive, they compared websites on their phones, texted their mates and discussed what they didn't see on television. Neither ever watches television because it is far more authentic and, like, better, to watch box sets of *The Wire* and *Mad Men* than to watch them on telly. If you are not watching box sets you can download everything onto your laptop and watch it there. Anyway, why would you pay a television license when you don't need a license for a laptop?

They consulted the whisky list. Steve had a glass of Nikka whisky from Japan and Emma had a glass of Black Ram from Bulgaria. While chatting, they, like, amazingly, discovered that they had both done Australia and both had stopped off at Krabi in Thailand on the way back. They were both on a long boat on the same day exactly two years apart. They had almost met. OMG. But now Australia is over-run with tourists and backpackers so they would rather go to, say, Belize for an authentic experience. They wondered at how they used to think Barcelona was cool. Madrid maybe or Seville in an emergency landing, but Barcelona was so over; wouldn't even crash land there.

They consulted the whisky list again. Steve had a Mackmyra whisky from Sweden and Emma had a Penderyn from Wales.

They were getting on so well together by this stage that they decided to bring a bottle of chardonnay, which is back in in Dublin 8 after being out in Dublin 4, to a BYO[29] in the closed-down art gallery space across the road from the jail on Arbour Hill. Whatshisname, who was with the whatdoyoucallems, was having a free gig to launch his solo career on the balalaika.

Emma told me that the rest of the night was none of my fucking business. If I ever told anyone, especially Steve, that they had gotten together for research, she would kill me. She wouldn't even tell me if they were going to meet again.

Thinking Like Hegel

If you can't find anything cool to carry around, not even a metallic lunch-box signifying your ironic relationship to heavy labour, and no one cool will go out with you, you can resort to the last rule of being cool. Sit around a café reading post-modern criticism; criticism of anything will do. You can apply post-modern theory to practically anything you are not doing at that time. Foucault is as passé as The Eagles, though you might hesitantly refer to his *Histories of Sexuality* as if you read all three volumes. Derrida, Deleuze, Guattari, Kristeva and Bhabha are as over as leg warmers. Leg warmers are ambiguous. When you see them on someone on the bus, you wonder whether they are on the way back in or if the wearer may have just been released from a very long prison sentence. Only be seen reading these post-modern critics if you can prove you haven't been detained at the expense of the State. You can pass off Baudrillard and Bourdieu as ironic reading only in the original French. Have Slavoj Zizek to hand only as a prelude to your Zizek story. When someone asks why you are reading that, say, 'When I

---

[29] In case you are uncool, BYO means bring your own bottle of wine.

met Slavoj in The Stags Head last week, he told me blah, blah blah...'. But you cannot go wrong with Hegel's *Phänomenologie des Geistes* in the original German. Tell people you have done with the contemporary because you have gone back to revisit the father of post-modern continental thought. You won't find anyone who has read it so you can feel free to give café lectures on German Idealism. How cool is that!

The inverse rules on how to be cool are also valid. If you have a well-paid responsible job in genetic engineering and you read the *Indo*, you are definitely not cool.

Not Being Cool: How to Be GAA

If you live outside Dublin or have migrated into Dublin from the countryside, you may be finding it difficult to live with the pressures of trying to be hip. Help is at hand in the form of the Gaelic Athletic Association, which was founded in the late nineteenth century to cater for the needs of people who are not cool, know they are not and don't care: basically everyone living outside Dublin 8 and 6W. Currently, it is easily the biggest organisation in the country. It was originally formed as an amateur organisation for the promotion of Gaelic Games, specifically hurling, Gaelic football and camogie, which is hurling played by women.

The Rules for Joining the GAA

The GAA is not just for exercise. It provides an outlet for a range of social interactions: screaming at the referee, analysing past games and testing your memory against other members, practising your ability to sit on committees and refining bureaucratic procedures. If you prove to be a hopeless player, you can become an authority on the game and how it should be played, particularly in hurling. In order to be truly Irish, never mind learning to step dance, play the fiddle or speak Irish. Join the GAA. But first you have to learn the rules. Because the GAA has strict entry criteria, not everyone will qualify.

The Rules of Hurling on the Ditch

We know from anthropology that the behaviour of fans is culturally determined. We know from the GAA that their fans achieve the apotheosis of Irish experience. To be a great GAA fan takes practice, practice and more practice. You can practise at home in front of the telly before going public on the terraces. Just before the match begins, make yourself a large traditional bacon sandwich with two slices of over-sized grinder, to be consumed with a large mug of tea or fifteen cans of Guinness. From the first whistle of the match, you should hurl abuse as loudly as you can at the television. Aim to be heard by the neighbours five houses away. Invite witnesses around to visit, place them on the couch beside you, offer them a can and then ignore them. Carry a cloth for wiping the spit and crumbs off the television screen. You should ask the GAA membership steward, who will have arrived with his clipboard to assess your application as a fan, to sit in the corner out of line of sight of the telly and 'to shush' while the match is on. Accepted commentary, which can be shouted by you in any order without reference to specific action, includes:

> 'For fuck's sake ref, get a pair of fucking glasses.'
> 'Get up you lazy whore.'
> 'Get up the fucking field.'
> 'It wouldn't be a Munster final without a brawl.'
> 'For Jaysus sake, that's a penalty, ref.'
> 'Ya bollocks, get your man. GET YOUR MAN. Ah, feck.'
> 'Where did that go? Did anyone see where that ball went? I don't believe it. It's in the back of the fucking net.'

'Stop acting the mickey and get up off the ground.'

'Things are looking good – they have the breeze behind them now.'

'Drive the ball up the field, ya hoor.'

'I'd say that's a line ball. That's a line ball, ye feckin' blind bat.'

'Free out. FREE OUT, ya blind bastard.'

'He's up. He's down. He's up again.'

'Over the bar is the place for that ball.'

'Take him on. TAKE HIM ON!'

The second part of your assessment for fandom takes place that evening in the pub, where you should briefly discuss the match you saw that day, before moving on to the more important topic of discussing every club, county or inter-county game that a) you attended or some member of your family attended on your behalf in the last month, and b) that took place during the last seventy-five years. Novice fans are allowed to discuss games within a ten-year period.

Not everyone can be a supporter. In order to be a true supporter, you need to have an infallible memory for all the teams and actual individual games since the GAA was founded. Well, actually that isn't true. Just pretend that you remember everything. As no one else remembers anything either, they won't have the confidence to actually contradict you. If they say, 'You haven't a feckin' clue what you are talking about,' they are not challenging your memory or knowledge, they are just making conversation. You should keep going with your memories regardless. Most supporters don't remember their own names the morning after a big win. However, beware the supporters of teams that never win. Their memories of games are probably still intact.

Starting with an uneven year, begin thus:

'Do you remember the Munster final in Thurles in 1937.' Pause and look around. If anyone nods and looks wistfully out the window in a reverie of recall, quickly interrupt yourself and say, 'Thirty-five, it was thirty-five. Jaysus, that was a great game. They don't make players like that anymore.' All nod in agreement. Allow someone else to develop the plot.

'Is that the game where Billy Barry played on for twenty minutes after his leg broke?'

'Broke! It was cut clean off just below the knee and he played on. Scored two points.' And on you go. It's improv really.

If your team actually wins a game, you need to be ready to react to that appropriately. You can start your analysis of the winning performance by referencing last year's failed efforts. It is unusual for a team to win in consecutive years, given the burden of mandatory celebrations that last well into the season following a victory. To join in the conversation amongst fans, you can say, 'We got bate last year but we came back this year and won it. Our lads looked after themselves all through the terrible winter. They came out for the training on a night when you wouldn't have shoved your cat outside for a shite. Our players didn't care what they went through to get this win. But they didn't do it for themselves. They did it for us, the people of this county. They played some fierce football. They played their hearts out.' At this point you should start crying.

Following the perfection of your commentary at home and having built up your confidence in the pub with a virtuoso display of memory, you can apply to go public on the terraces. The following traditional comments will allow you to make a convincing impression on your fellow fans. Say the following authentic GAA phrases to whoever you find yourself beside at the match:

'It's coming into the busy time of the year as everyone knows.'
'There was huge disappointment when our side lost.'

'We lost because the other team were better on the day.'

'We didn't match our expectations on the day.'

'It was a hard winter because winters are hard.'

'Training was tough because training is very tough.'

'The commitment of our team is always one hundred and ten per cent.'

'It's going to be a great campaign because we have a great group of lads with big hearts [not a symptom of coronary disease].'

'Tipperary people are hurling people.'

'Kilkenny people are hurling people.'

'People who don't hurl don't know what they are talking about.'

'I am always disappointed when something doesn't happen, unless it is something that I am happy happened, like winning against the run of play.'

'I am delighted but all credit has to go to the group of fantastic lads.'

'From a personal point of view it won't affect me.'

'There is a hunger there [nothing to do with crowds at the chip van].'

The Rules of Interviewing Stars

To secure your reputation as a die-hard GAA supporter, you should interview your favourite player after the match for your local parish newspaper or blog. Stick with the obvious questions and ask nothing tricky. Here are a few standard questions that will get the ball rolling (punning is usually mandatory).

Q: Will playing with a broken arm and leg and a burst spleen have any effect on your game in next Saturday's semi-final?

A: No, it won't, because it is always an honour to play with this group of lads. They all give one hundred and ten per cent. I am disappointed when I can't give one hundred and ten per cent but I'll be giving it one hundred per cent with the arm and leg I have left. What is a spleen used for anyway?

Q: When ye went twenty-six goals and forty-three points down in the first twenty minutes, did that upset your game plan to pull off the draw?

A: No, no, not really. They had the breeze behind them. It's all part of the game. I knew we would get a fair bit of stick at half-time, but we fought back valiantly. They were the better team on the day. Never mind your games. It's the replays that count.

Q: Losing twenty-two years in a row must have undermined your confidence?

A: Not at all. It only made me more determined to give one hundred and ten per cent.

How to Become a Referee

If you are super uncool, you might qualify to be a referee. If you want to be considered for refereeing, you should fail an eye test and send written confirmation of this condition to GAA headquarters in Croke Park. Next, you should turn up for interview sporting a pair of jam-jar glasses. Usefully, the GAA publishes a list of attributes that will make you a good referee. You should *have a thorough knowledge of the rules*. As these are changed every season, knowing them is a life-long commitment. But while refereeing a match, to keep the fans happy you should ironically display no familiarity with whatever rules are current. You should *be physically and mentally fit*, which will allow you to escape the stampeding crowd by having the wit to run towards an exit, as soon as the match is over. You should *deal courteously with players and officials*. For example, as you run towards the exit ask the goalie can he please remind you where you parked your car. You should *have the ability to remain calm* when hiding in a locker in the dressing room. You should *operate strictly in accordance with the principles of justice and fair play,* which means that you should not bring charges against the fathers of the under-ten side who ran amok. Similarly, you should *have the moral courage to take decisions which are correct,* which means don't bring charges against the mothers either. You should *be able to live with unfair criticism* and threats against your life. You should *be able to accept constructive criticism,* such as on the marital status of your mother or the sums your sister is charging for her affections. You should *retain a good learning graph,* which I think is a type of hairstyle. You should *be alert and decisive on the field,* which means knowing exactly when to escape. You should *enjoy refereeing,* which means not dealing with the other major issues in your life that have driven you to it. You should *be committed to the protection of players and the prevention of abusive or violent conduct.* This means that you should supply your own security arrangements. You should be *a good communicator on and off the field.* A characteristic that separates great referees from the herd is their reluctance to go toe-to-toe with the crowd in an abuse-hurling competition. You should *behave with dignity both on and off the field,* which is helped by the use of disguises when off the field. Above all things else, *you must retain integrity, consistency and uniformity.* I assume that this is what you wear on the pitch.

* * *

As you put on more and more weight, you will find yourself slipping out of your cool circles. You may have even fallen into a relationship with someone on the Northside who actually makes money from doing something with their hands. Soon you will only see your old cool friends from the car on your way to the MacDonald's drive thru on the Naas Road. Imagine you once ate at Rick's Burgers on Dame St. When obese and totally uncool, you will be spotted at a Dickie

Rock concert in the Red Cow Hotel, where you went to meet newly discovered relations from Cork who were afraid to drive to your house in Cabra.

When you are no longer cool because you have been away from the Dublin 8 scene for too long, you will end up in The Big Tree pub wearing a Meath County football jersey.

Glossary

Dáil	The Irish parliament
ESB	Electricity Supply Board
Fianna Fáil	Centrist political party
Fine Gael	Centre-right to centrist political party; currently the largest political party in Ireland
GAA	Gaelic Athletic Association
Garda/Guard	A member of An Garda Síochána
An Garda Síochána	The Irish police force
TD	Teachta Dála, which is Irish for a member of parliament